Anyone who is considering staging a full production of this film/play, may, for the same cost of this book purchase a full copy of the script in double spaced and A4 format, for the purposes of either script reading, or rehearsals, by simply contacting

maximilianrothschild@hotmail.co.uk/

fingerprintbooks@hotmail.co.uk

or by texting the scriptwriter/playwright,

D M Hopkins
on
07810 722375

Scriptwriter/Playwright

D M HOPKINS

Would like to dedicate this film/play
to David and Donny,
Who have always been kind enough to support
and encourage him over the years.

Front cover Donny
Back cover David

Covers designed by 'The Hopkins Gallery'

'the songwriter'

film/play

by

D M Hopkins

First Edition Published in 2011 by Maximilian Rothschild
Apartment 1
55 Rye Hill Park Peckham Rye London SE15 3JN

All rights reserved
© D M Hopkins 2011

The right of D M Hopkins to be identified as author of this work has been asserted in accordance with section 77 of the Copyright, Design and Patents Act 1988.

This book is sold subject to the condition that it shall not by way of trade or otherwise, be lent, resold, hired out or otherwise circulated without the publisher's prior consent in any form of binding or cover other than that in which it is published and without a similar condition including this condition being imposed on the subsequent purchaser.

A CIP record for this book is available from the British Library

Printed by Copyzone Limited
Unit 3, Southmill Trading Centre Southmill Road
Bishop's Stortford CM23 3DY

ISBN 978 0 9566536 2 8

maximilianrothschild@hotmail.co.uk

fingerprintbooks@hotmail.co.uk

scriptwriter/playwright D M Hopkins

text to 07810-722375

Maximilian Rothschild

Maximilian Rothschild

'the songwriter'

a film/play

by
D M Hopkins

'the songwriter'

a film/play

by D M Hopkins

Synopsis:

Ricky Beaumont wants to be a songwriter but his dad has other ideas. Ricky also falls head over heels in love with the factory 'bike' and is the only one who can't see that she is just simply using him to make her steady boyfriend, Johnny Watson, jealous.

Fights, drugs, drink and unemployment threaten to tear the family apart. Stella (Ricky's elder sister) fights to save her little brother from the little tart, who tries her best to split the family up and break poor Ricky's heart.

Will Ricky's dad ever come back home, or will Ricky take his own life? Perhaps he'll become a famous songwriter and simply find himself a wife.

There's comedy, violence and love in every scene, so to find out more, read the script, scene, by scene, by scene.

'the songwriter'

CAST:

RICKY BEAUMONT

DOT BEAUMONT

JACK BEAUMONT

STELLA BEAUMONT

JENNY BEAUMONT

JOHNNY WATSON

SHEILA BURTON

BRIAN COOPER

ETHEL LAKINS

MR DICKENS

NORMAN WATSON

MRS BURTON

MR BURTON

CAROL

KATE

KAREN

MR SOIZA

MISS PETERS

ASHLEY

MANDY AND DIANA
(SHEILA'S MATES)

JANET, MARY AND BURT

RICKY'S MATES
MICKEY, PETE, BARRY AND TONY

JOHNNY'S MATES
DAVE, JOEY, TERRY AND STEVE

FACTORY WORKERS

'the songwriter'

by D M Hopkins

Description of cast:

In the play version, most of the main cast will also be expected to double up as: factory workers, café customers and locals in the pub scenes.

RICKY: 15/16 years old, slim, medium height, scruffy, good-looking and very cheeky. He is kind, but no mug. A bit of a romantic I suppose, who wants something better in his life than going down the local pit or working in a factory.

DOT: 35/40 years old, slim, petite, and very motherly. Works hard to bring her family up properly, with very little money and hates what her husband has become, but understands why! She is simply a loving mother, who hopes for better things.

JACK: 40/45 years old and is a very attractive man for is age. He is strong, proud and has been a hard-working father and a good husband, who, sadly, has now lost his sense of direction in life due to unemployment.

Continued:

STELLA: Is a sexy, tall, nice looking 19 year-old, who has a good figure. Outspoken, bossy, very stroppy and doesn't suffer fools very easily. She tries hard to help her mum to keep the family together, by keeping her brother Ricky in line. She has a hard shell, with a soft centre!

JENNY: Funny, dizzy, lazy and doesn't let things bother her too much. 17 years old, quiet compared to her elder sister and hates arguments. She's not bad looking, but she's skinny and doesn't have much dress sense; a bit of a Goth I suppose.

JOHNNY: He's tall, dark and handsome. He is also tough and has lots of sex appeal for a 20 year old factory worker. A big hit with the ladies, and has a good collection of mates. (Jack the lad.)

SHEILA: Very attractive, but she's a bit of a tart. She also likes to play the field and to tease all the boys. 20 years old and already knows that she is the pick of the litter. She likes wearing very short mini-skirts, low cut tops and high-heel shoes.

BRIAN: Middle-aged, funny, easy going, likes a pint and makes a good friend. I suppose that he's just a little bit on the slow side, in a comical way. Oh, and he also likes the ladies!

Continued:

ETHEL: 45/50 years old, and Dot's best friend. She's kind, understanding and wants to help if she can. She likes to gossip over a cup of tea, but there's no real harm in her.

NORMAN: The factory foreman, and also Johnny's dad. He's tall and skinny, about 40 and a bit of a drip, but he also has a good sense of humour.

MRS BURTON: Sheila's mum is about 35 years old. She's very common, loud mouthed and also swears quite a lot. Plus she speaks her mind. (In other words, she's not to be messed with.)

MR BURTON: Sheila's dad is in his mid forties, he is fat, extremely loud and very aggressive. Plus the actor playing Mr Burton also plays the part of Mr Dickens, the factory manager, who has a (comical sounding) high-pitched voice.

CAROL: Is the main barmaid. She is 19, very attractive, sexy, and has a really nice figure. Plus she's also got a good head on her shoulders.

KATE: Who plays the second barmaid, Is a somewhat plain 18-year old, who is also quite cheeky. She also plays a factory worker and one of Ricky's mate's girlfriends.

Continued:

MR SOIZA: Is in his late twenties and turns out to be a surprisingly good friend, from out of Jack's past. He is Spanish, and looks every bit of it, with his dark hair and dark brown eyes. He is also tall, well dressed and well spoken.

MISS PETERS: 30/35 Personnel Officer. She is stuck up, patronising and she is definitely not a very sympathetic person.

ASHLEY: 18 years old, nice looking, posh, well educated, and she also has a nice little figure.

JANET, MARY AND BURT: Are in their forties. Janet is sex mad and works in the factory with her best friend Mary. Burt is Mary's husband. All are loud and common, but are nice people.

THREE OF RICKY'S MATES: 15/17 years old and all very energetic and leery. They are funny, and are always playing around and taking the piss out of each other.

FACTORY WORKERS: Male and female of mixed age groups. All like a laugh and to have a bit of fun; some obviously have bigger parts to play than others.

The entire cast will be expected to double up as factory works and coffee bar customers

                                          D M Hopkins

I HOPE YOU WILL
ENJOY READING, OR WATCHING
'THE SONGWRITER', AS MUCH
AS I HAVE ENJOYED WRITING IT.

Scriptwriter/Playwright D M Hopkins

'the songwriter'

'the songwriter'
a film and a play by D M Hopkins

ACT 1

SCENE 1   (LIVING ROOM)

'TRYING TO WATCH TELEVISION'

Scene one opens in the living room of a small Victorian terraced house, where we can clearly hear very loud music coming from the direction of the attic bedroom, which is being played by Ricky, who is the youngest member of the household. Ricky shares the house with his mum, dad and two elder sisters, Stella and Jenny. The problem is Ricky's music is now so loud that Jack, the boy's father, simply can't take it any more and has finally snapped, leaving Dot, Ricky's mum, to have to do her best to try and calm the situation down. We find Jack standing at the bottom of the stairs, where he is shouting at the top of his voice, for Ricky to turn it down.

JACK: (*Angrily*) For *Christ's sake* Ricky, turn that flamin' racket down before I come up there and put mi foot through the bloody thing. (*Beat*) Did you hear what I said?

Now either Ricky can't hear him, or he's simply ignoring him. Dot (Mrs Beaumont and the boy's mother) comes into the hall from the kitchen area of the room, to investigate what all the shouting is about.

DOT: Now what's up wi' ya' and what's all the bloody shoutin' about this time?

JACK: What's up? I'll tell ya' what's up shall I? Just listen to that racket up there. I mean, 'ave you ever heard anythin' like it in ya' life? 'Cos God only knows what the neighbours must think!

Dot tries to calm things down, as she takes hold of Jack's arm and gently coaxes him back into the living room.

DOT: Hey! Come on luv; leave the lad alone and bugger the bloody neighbours, 'cos who the hell cares what they think, anyway. (*Beat*) That's right, you come and sit yersen down and watch ya' football, while I make us both a nice cup a tea.

So Jack sits down and watches the football on the television, while Dot exits into the kitchen to put the kettle on.

JACK: What's he doin' up there anyway, that's what I'd like to know? The noisy little bugger!

DOT: Now, ya' know very well what he's doin'. Only he's practisin' one of the new songs that he's just written, 'cos one day he wants to be a songwriter like John Lennon and...

JACK: *A songwriter!* Hey, I'll give him *bloody* songwriter, 'cos it's about time he got down to some serious studyin' and then he might at least stand a chance of gettin' into a decent university, instead of muckin' about up there all flamin' day, writin' stupid bloody songs.

DOT: Now look, ya' 'ave to try and...

JACK: 'Cos all he's doin' is wastin' his time, but ya' know that don't ya'? Just wastin' his flamin' time!

DOT: Yes, but if you'd just...

JACK: *Songwriter!* Bloody songwriter my arse, 'cos that's not a proper flamin' job, now is it?

Dot fetches the tea and puts it down on the table in front of him, just as the music suddenly starts to become even louder than it was before.

Right, that's it! Only I've had just about as much as I can take for one day.

Jack shoots off up the stairs like a rocket to Ricky's bedroom, which is right up at the top of the house, in the attic.

END OF SCENE 1

SET CHANGE   (BEDROOM AND LANDING)

SCENE 2

'UP IN RICKY'S BEDROOM'

Jack bursts into Ricky's room and yanks the amplifier plug clean out of the wall socket. The music stops instantly!

RICKY: *Hey!* What the *bloody hell* did ya' do that for, ya' stupid prat?

Short pause (as Jack is too out of breath to reply, after having to climb up all those stairs.)

JACK: What did I do that for? (*Pauses for breath*) I'll tell ya' what I did that for, shall I. (*Pauses for breath*) It's 'cos it's too *bloody* loud and what's more, (*Pauses for breath*) it sounds flamin' awful.

RICKY: But I'm practisin' one of mi new songs.

JACK: Well, I wouldn't bother if I were you, (*Pauses for breath*) 'cos from what I've heard, the flamin' cat could do it better!

Ricky, who is obviously not amused, just stands there glaring at him.

RICKY: Oh yeah, very funny, but ya' won't be sayin' that when I'm a famous songwriter, will ya?

Jack bursts out laughing.

JACK: What, you, a famous songwriter! (*Pause for breath*), Don't make mi laugh, 'cos let's face it, ya' can't even write a flamin' letter properly, (*Pause for breath*) never mind tryin' to write stupid bloody songs. I mean, just who the *hell* do ya' think ya' are? Paul McCartney?

Ricky throws his microphone down on the bed.

RICKY: *Oi!* One day I'll be a famous songwriter and 'ave lots of money. (*Beat*) No, I won't be stuck on the bloody dole like you, borrowin' money off of anybody and everybody, just 'cos ya' too thick to go out and get yersen a bleedin' job!

On hearing this, Jack is left somewhat speechless once again for a couple of seconds.

JACK: Well until ya' do, Mr *Bloody Know-It-All*, then you'd better start to turn it down a little bit, if ya' know what's good for ya'.

Jack leaves, slamming the door behind him, as he starts to go back downstairs. So, now feeling safe, Ricky sticks two fingers up at him.

I saw that Ricky Beaumont.

RICKY: (*Looking puzzled*) Er... How the *hell* did he...

Shaking his head, Ricky quickly plugs the amp back in and starts singing again, albeit a lot quieter this time. Now as Jack is making his way back down the second floor landing, he bumps into (Ricky's elder sister) Stella, who is coming out of the bathroom, in nothing but her underwear as usual.

STELLA: Hey, what's up wi' you? (*Beat*) Only, don't tell mi that our Ricky's bin windin' ya' up *again!*

JACK: My good God Stella, if it's not you, then it's our Jenny. Only for *Christ's sake* stop runnin' about the house in just yer bra and panties, will ya'?

STELLA: *Oi!* Don't go takin' it out on me dad, just 'cos our Ricky's bin givin' ya' a hard time!

JACK: Now you listen to me young lady, 'cos it's gettin' to be just like a Mexican brothel in here at times. What wi' you and our Jenny, always goin' about the house in ya' flamin' underwear all the time.

STELLA: Er... Hang on a minute. How would you know what a Mexican brothel looks like? (*Beat*) Unless...

JACK: Hey, never you mind young lady and don't ya' be so bloody cheeky.

Just then, (Stella's younger sister) Jenny, also comes out of the bathroom and all she's wearing is a black G-string, with no bra on at all. So as you can imagine, her more than ample breasts are bouncing about all over the place, leaving poor Jack to have to try and do his best not to look.

JACK: And that goes for you as well, our Jenny. So, for *goodness sake* put some flippin' clothes on can't ya', 'cos there's men in this house, ya' know?

JENNY: (*Laughing*) Oh, is there? Hey, that's great dad. So, where are they, 'cos I've not seen 'um, 'ave you, Stel?

END OF SCENE 2

SET CHANGE   (BEDROOM AND BATHROOM)

SCENE 3

'TIME TO GET UP FOR WORK'

The next morning, Dot is at the bottom of the stairs, where she is trying her best to get Ricky to get up and go to work.

We don't see Dot, we only hear her voice.

DOT: *Ricky!* It's time ya' were gettin' up, or ya' gonna' be late for work luv.

There's no reply.

Did ya' hear what I said, Ricky? (*There's still no reply.*)

Ricky!

STELLA: (*Shouts downstairs*) It's alright mam, you leave it to us, 'cos we'll soon get the lazy little bugger out of bed.

So, Stella and Jenny, who are still only wearing their bra and panties, quietly make their way into Ricky's bedroom. They then take hold of Ricky's bedclothes and pull them all off onto the floor, but this has no effect on Ricky whatsoever. So lifting up one side of the mattress, they tip him out onto the floor.

RICKY: *Oi!* What the *bloody hell* did ya' do that for, ya' stupid idiots?

Getting up off the floor, Ricky then chases them both out of his bedroom and into the bathroom, where they quickly lock the door behind them.

Hey, you just wait, 'cos I'll get mi own back on ya'. You see if I don't.

JENNY: (*Laughing*) Oh, we're really scared of ya', aren't wi Stella?

STELLA: Yeah, ya' really frightenin' me, Ricky.

RICKY: Sisters, *bloody* sisters! Who needs 'um anyway?

Going back into his bedroom, Ricky grabs hold of the side of his mattress and, after a bit of a struggle, eventually manages to pull it back onto the bed. Then he is just getting back into bed and starting to pull the blankets back up over him, when who should come storming into his room but his dad, who it has to be said, doesn't look all that pleased with him.

JACK: Hey, now come on lad, let's be havin' ya'. 'Cos God only knows what you'd a done, if you'd a worked at pit and got to be at Whaleybrook Colliery for 5 o'clock in't mornin'.

RICKY: Well, it didn't do ya' much good, did it?

JACK: No, but it didn't do mi any *bloody* harm either, ya' cheeky little bugger. So come on, let's 'ave ya' gettin' ya' backside off that bed and gettin' off to flamin' work, before I stick mi boot up ya' arse. (*Beat*) Now, *come on!*

Jack then storms out of the room. So Ricky decides that he'd better get dressed and go downstairs for his breakfast, before his dad ends up bursting a blood vessel.

END OF SCENE 3

SET CHANGE   (DINING KITCHEN)

SCENE 4

'IN THE DINING KITCHEN'

Dot, Stella and Jenny, are already sitting at the kitchen table eating their breakfasts when Ricky walks in.

DOT: Oh, there you are! Now, come on Ricky luv, hurry up, or ya' gonna' be late for ya' first day at work and ya' don't want that now do ya'?

Ricky immediately starts to do an impression of his dad, to the obvious amusement of both his sisters.

RICKY: Hey, when I worked at Whaleybrook pit, I had to get up before I went to bed, and walk thirty miles in mi bare feet and all I had for mi breakfast were a belt round ear-hole off of mi dad.

Stella and Jenny burst out laughing

DOT: *Listen!* You'd better not let ya' dad catch ya' talkin' like that or you'll be for it mi lad.

RICKY: Now look mam, I know that mi dad went to a lot of trouble to get mi this job, but the truth is I don't want it. 'Cos I want to be a famous songwriter.

STELLA: Oh, get you! *Hey,* and I wanted to be a fashion model, but look at me. I'm havin' to work as a waitress down at the Four Seasons coffee bar.

RICKY: What, you, a model? What, wi' an arse like yours?

Stella starts chasing Ricky round and round the kitchen table to shrieks of laughter from Jenny.

STELLA: Why ya' cheeky little bugger, ya' just wait till I get mi hands on ya'.

'the songwriter'

RICKY: (*Laughing*) Hey listen, the only model you'll ever be is an Airfix Lancaster Bomber.

This only makes Jenny laugh even louder and even Dot can't help having a little smile.

DOT: Now look, you'd all better get ya' breakfasts down ya' and get off to work before ya' dad comes down, or I can tell ya' now that there'll be trouble.

JENNY: *Trouble!* But I 'aven't done anythin' wrong mam, so why...

Jack suddenly comes bursting into the kitchen.

JACK: *Oi!* What's all the *bloody* noise about, 'cos they can hear ya' halfway down the flamin' street.

So not wanting any trouble, they all finish off their breakfasts and then quickly get off to work, as Dot hands them all their lunchboxes.

STELLA: Bye mam, see ya' later?

DOT: Yes, bye luv, take care.

JACK: Hey, and you'd better not be late for work either, Ricky.

RICKY: (*Under his breath*) *Piss off!*

JACK: What did ya' just say?

RICKY: *Nothin'!*

As soon as they've gone out of the door, Jack puts his arms around Dot's waist and they start dancing around the kitchen floor singing to the music of 'You've lost that loving feeling.'

DOT: (*Sighs*) Oh, I really enjoyed that luv, 'cos it's been a long time since you've sung to mi like that and you've got a lovely voice, ya' know. (*Beat*) Er... I've just had a thought; perhaps that's where our Ricky gets it all from.

JACK: Hey now look, I know ya' busy and all that, but ya' don't fancy a bit of ya' know what do ya'? Ya' know, now that we've finally got the house to ourselves.

DOT: (*Shaking her head*) Well, you certainly didn't waste any time, did ya?' It's just I wondered why ya' were so eager to get our Ricky out to work, ya' crafty devil.

JACK: So, what about it then?

DOT: (*Sighs*) Aye, alright then, but ya' gonna' 'ave to wait until I've finished washin' these pots though.

JACK: Er... I tell ya' what. Why don't ya' leave the washin' up for now and I'll do 'em for ya' later, if ya' like.

DOT: *Blimey!* Ya' must really want it bad luv, 'cos you've never offered to wash the pots for mi before, 'ave ya'?

JACK: Hey, wi could 'ave it on't end of kitchen table if ya' like? (*Beat*) Ya' know, like wi used to do, when wi first got married.

DOT: (*Laughing*) On't end of kitchen... (*Beat*) Well, you've certainly got a bloody good memory, Jack Beaumont. I'll say that for ya.'

JACK: Well, what do ya' think?

DOT: Aye, alright, go on then, 'cos I could do wi' a bloody good laugh.

Dot lifts up her skirt and pulls down her knickers, then she sits down on the end of the kitchen table with her back to the audience, and they start making love. However, while Jack is making love to her, Dot is constantly bringing up the subject of Ricky not wanting to go to work at the factory, which isn't going down very well at all with Jack. In fact, if anything, it's putting him right off his stroke.

DOT: Oh, and by the way, our Ricky's not very happy about havin' to work down at the factory ya' know 'cos he says he wants to be a songwriter.'

JACK: Aye, but which silly bugger put that daft idea into his head, that's what I'd like to know?

DOT: Now look, he's only a young lad, so why don't ya' let the lad 'ave his dreams, 'cos it won't do him any harm and ya' never know, he might even pull it off.

JACK: Er... Ya' are jokin', aren't ya'? I mean, our Ricky, a songwriter? Don't make mi laugh!

DOT: Hey, why don't ya' try and give the lad a little bit of support for once, instead of puttin' him down all the time?

Jack is really beginning to get annoyed now because Dot is constantly going on about Ricky wanting to be a songwriter.

JACK: Oh for *Christ's sake* Dot, can't ya' think of anythin' better to talk about? (*Beat*) 'Cos ya' spoilin' the mood.

DOT: Yes, well I know all about that! But this is the only time that I can get ya' full attention these days.

JACK: Er... I tell ya' what! You'd better not let mi catch ya' puttin' any of these daft ideas into his head, or I'll...

Dot suddenly pushes him away from her, as Jack is then left to have to quickly pull up his trousers.

DOT: Yes, go on say it, or you'll what?

So now sensing a big argument, Jack decides not to say any more about it.

END OF SCENE 4

SET CHANGE   (FACTORY/PRODUCTION LINE)

SCENE 5

'RICKY GOES TO WORK'

At the factory, Ricky meets with the foreman who is in charge of the production line that he's going to be working on.

'the songwriter'

NORMAN: (*The foreman*) Right Ricky, follow me 'cos I'm going to put ya' on the production line wi' one of the other young lads, so that he can show ya' the ropes. Now, if ya' get any problems, or if ya' get stuck, then all you've got to do is gimme a shout, okay?

RICKY: Yeah, alright.

Ricky is led over to the production line.

NORMAN: Oi, Tony! This is that new lad I was tellin' ya' about. You know, Ricky Beaumont. So, do mi a favour will ya' and just keep an eye on him for mi. *Alright!*

TONY: Aye, alright, Norm but I'm not 'is *bloody* nursemaid ya' know?

NORMAN: Now look, don't go start all that up again, or I'll stick ya' back on the flamin' night shift where ya' belong!

Exit Norman, shaking his head.

Pete, one of the other lads that works on the production line, immediately recognises Ricky as Jenny's younger brother.

PETE: Er... Wait a minute. You're Jenny Beaumont's little brother, aren't ya?

RICKY: (*Snaps at him*) Well, what if I am? What's it got to do wi' you anyway?

PETE: Hey, watch it ya' cheeky little sod or I'll land ya' one. (*Beat*) It's just that I've always had a soft spot for your Jenny and so I wouldn't mind takin' her out to the pictures one night, if she'd let mi.

RICKY: *Ya' what!* Listen, you've got no chance mate, 'cos our Jenny wouldn't be seen dead wi' a prat like you.

TONY: Oi you two, pack it in and come and take a look at what's just come out of the office. 'Cos it's none other than, Sheila *hot lips* Burton herself. (*Beat*) *Wow!* I wouldn't mind takin' her out one night and teachin' her the facts of life.

'the songwriter'

A young girl in a short miniskirt can now be seen coming out of the office, carrying a stack of heavy paperwork. Mary, one of the older women that works on the production line starts laughing as she shouts across to Janet, one of her workmates.

MARY: Oh, hark at the voice of experience, Janet. I mean, it were only a few days ago that he found out what it was really for and I don't mean *pissin'!*

TONY: Hey, I'll tell thee what, Scary Mary. If ya' were the only woman left on this earth, then that's all I bloody well would use it for, *pissin'!*

JANET: Why ya' cheeky little bugger, you just wait until I see ya' mam down at the bingo on Saturday night.

TONY: Well listen, don't forget to take ya' bus passes wi' ya', 'cos they're lettin' old age pensioners in for nothin' now, on Saturday nights.

Jumping up, Janet starts to chase him out of the room, to loud cheers and laughter from all the other women.

JANET: Ya' just wait, Tony Warren, 'cos I'll get mi own back on ya' sooner or later! Ya' cheeky little sod.

By now, the young girl from out of the office is about halfway across the factory floor, as all the boys stop work and begin to crowd round her. They then start to tease her and take the Mickey, as she tries hard to escape, but she can't because she is now completely trapped inside a circle of young boys.

Ricky liked her the moment he set eyes on her, so after all the other boys have got bored with her and gone back to work, he decides to follow her down to the end of the production line, where after some initial nerves, Ricky, eventually manages to pluck up enough courage to ask her out on a date.

RICKY: (*Nervously*) Hey, Sheila, do ya' fancy comin' out wi' mi on Friday night to't pictures?

Sheila laughs at first and is just about to reply, when a very attractive well-built guy suddenly appears on the scene.

It's Johnny Watson, who unbeknown to Ricky, also happens to be Sheila's steady boyfriend.

JOHNNY: *Oi!* What the *bloody hell's* goin' on here? Only is this little *toerag* givin' ya' any trouble, Babe?

Sheila puts down her paperwork and rushes over to Johnny's side, because she knows what will happen if she doesn't.

SHEILA: Who, him! No, he's just a kid, that's all. So come on, let's go out the back for a bit of fun, before anybody has a chance to miss me.

She then pulls Johnny out through one of the side doors, into the yard at the side of the factory, just as Ricky's foreman comes in and spots him standing about doing nothing. So, putting both his hands up to his mouth like a megaphone, his foreman starts to bellow at him at the top of his voice.

NORMAN: *Oi!* What the *hell* do ya' think this is? A *bloody* holiday camp? Now come on, first day, or no first day, let's 'ave ya' back on this production line, *now!*

MARY: Hey, they don't want work, Norman, I'll tell ya.'
In fact, they're just bone-idle, the whole bleedin' lot of 'em. 'Cos if it were left up to me; I wouldn't pay 'em in flamin' washers.

JANET: Aye, and I'd make 'um all stay behind and finish off their work in their own time, if I had my way.

NORMAN: Oh, ya' would, would ya'? Well, I've got just one thing to say to you, Janet Baxter.

JANET: (*Laughing*) Oh, well this should be good anyway. (*Beat*) So go on then, what is it 'O wise and masterful one'?

NORMAN: Firm's annual day-trip to Skegness, on't back seat a bus! (*Beat*) Remember?

All the other women on the production line suddenly burst out laughing. And it's not long before everyone is joining in and having a really good laugh, at Janet's expense.

JANET: Oh, trust you to remember that bogger. It's just I'd a thought that everybody would 'ave forgotten all about that by now.

Janet begins to blush, as she quickly turns round and starts to get on with her work again.

NORMAN: *Forgotten about it!* Ya' are jokin', aren't ya'? No, I haven't forgotten about it, 'cos I've got a bloody good memory for that sort of thing, ya' know.

MARY: Aye, well they say that elephants never forget, and your Missis once told me that you'd only got a *little tail.*

Well, while all this is going on, Ricky quickly goes back and gets on with his work on the production line. You see, what he doesn't know is that Johnny also happens to be the foreman's son, so as you would expect, Johnny is allowed to get away with murder.

Ricky talks to Pete.

RICKY: Hey, Pete, that Sheila Burton's nice lookin' in't she? (*Beat*) Only I don't suppose ya' know where she lives, do ya'?

PETE: Yeah, she's a bit of alright is our Sheila. Although, I'd be careful if I were you, 'cos if Johnny ever catches ya' wi' is bird, then I wouldn't like to be in your shoes. *If* ya' know what I mean?

RICKY: Hey, don't worry about me, 'cos I can look after misen!

Pete looks across at some of the other lads, who start shaking their heads, but don't make any comment.

PETE: Oh well in that case, she lives at 47 Byron Street. Ya' know, up on the old Council Estate. (*Beat*) Hey, but don't go tellin' everybody that I told ya', will ya'?

RICKY: No, don't worry Pete 'cos I won't say anythin' to anybody.

PETE: Good, 'cos I don't want to go and get a good hidin' off, Johnny Watson, even if you do!

END OF SCENE 5

SET CHANGE   (BAR ROOM)

SCENE 6

'DOWN AT THE PUB'

Jack and his best friend, Brian, are having a pint and a chat in the local pub, while Carol, the barmaid, is earwigging on their conversation as usual.

BRIAN: Er... Is everybody alright at home then, Jack? Only ya' look a bit down, if ya' don't mind mi sayin' like?

JACK: Aye, not too bad I suppose. Although, our Ricky's bein' a pain in the arse at the moment, but otherwise it's not too bad.

BRIAN: *Who?* Your Ricky? Well, what's up wi' him then; only I've always got on wi' him alright, 'cos he seems like a nice enough lad to me.

JACK: Oh, ah he is. No, don't get mi wrong, he's a good lad is our Ricky. It's just that he's got this daft idea about wantin' to be a bloody songwriter.

BRIAN: So, what's wrong wi' that? It's just there's some bloody good money in that game ya' know, especially if ya' any good at it. I mean, look at that Lenin 'n' McCarthy, 'cos they've made a bloody fortune out of it, and good luck to 'em that's what I say.

Jack and Carol, the barmaid, both turn and look at Brian a bit puzzled like.

JACK: (*Scratching his head*) Who? Lenin 'n' McCarthy? Oh, ya' mean, Lennon 'n' McCartney, ya' daft bugger?

BRIAN: Aye, that's right, them 'un all.

'the songwriter'

CAROL: (*Sighing*) Well, at least *he* knows who he's talkin' about, Jack.

JACK: (*Laughing*) Aye, but I'll be buggered if anybody else does though.

BRIAN: So, what's up then? 'Cos in't your Ricky any good at this song writin' lark, then?

JACK: No, no, it's nothin' like that, 'cos some of the songs that he writes sound pretty good to me. Aye, he's definitely got a way wi' words, 'as our Ricky.

BRIAN: Well, what's the problem then?

JACK: Hey, now look, you know as well as I do, Brian, that how many of 'em ever make it in that game? What, one in every hundred thousand and that's only if they're lucky and even then it's all hit 'n' miss.

CAROL: Yes, but that's his choice though Jack, not yours 'cos ya' should let him 'ave is head luv, and then he'll find out for himsen. Only I can tell ya' now that he won't thank ya' for interferin'. Well, not if that's what he really wants to do.

BRIAN: Aye, she's right ya' know Jack.

JACK: (*Sighs*) Aye, maybe she is, Brian, but I want him to go to a decent university and get a good education, 'cos he can always prat about doin' his stupid *bloody* songwritin' as a flamin' hobby.

BRIAN: Er… Hang on a minute, Jack, 'cos correct mi if I'm wrong but I seem to remember that you were in a band when ya' were a young lad, weren't ya'? (*Beat*) Now, what was it that ya' were called?

JACK: Aye, that's right I was, and wi were called 'Jumpin' Jack Beaumont and the Frogs.'

BRIAN: Aye that's it; I remember now, 'cos I knew it had somethin' to do wi' frogs' legs.

Carol begins to laugh.

CAROL: Jumpin' Jack Beaumont and the...

BRIAN: It's right, Carol. Jack us't to wear this bright green jacket and all the other lads in the band us't to wear skin-tight jeans and big black frogman's flippers, didn't they Jack?

CAROL: What, you, in a Rock 'n' Roll Band, Jack? I don't believe it.

BRIAN: It's true, he us't to jump about on top of the tables, jumpin' from one to the other, and when he started shakin' his hips, all the young girls us't to go crazy. Especially that night when his belt snapped and his flippin' trousers fell down.

CAROL: Ya' jokin'! (*Beat*) Oh, I'd 'ave loved to 'ave seen that Jack. I really would!

JACK: Aye well, it were a long time ago now, Carol, and wi were just kids really!

There's a short pause.

CAROL: Ya' mean, like your Ricky?

There's another short pause as Jack looks at them both.

JACK: Yeah, now I think about it, I was about the same age as our Ricky then. Except, somehow, wi were a lot more like adults in them days, do ya' know what I mean, Brian?

BRIAN: Aye, wi were a lot more mature for us age in them days, weren't wi?

CAROL: (*Smiling*) Ya' mean, ya' thought ya' were?

It goes quiet for a few seconds, as Carol comes from behind the bar and bends down to pick something up off the floor. Carol, who has a very nice figure, is wearing a low cut top and a very short miniskirt. So, as you'd expect, Jack and Brian are having a good look at her cute little round bum and her long shapely legs. They look at each other and begin to gesture that she is a bit of hot stuff, which they do by making various mouth and hand movements, after which they start fingering the inside of their shirt collars.

BRIAN: *Phew!* It's gettin' a bit hot in here, in't it Jack?

JACK: Aye, too *bloody* hot for my likin'!

Carol stops what she's doing and then turns round to look at them both.

CAROL: Well, would ya' like mi to go and fetch the steps and open a window for ya', Brian? Only I could open one of them right up there at the very top, if ya' like?

BRIAN: Aye, ya' can if ya' like, Carol, 'cos perhaps one of them right up there at the very top might just let in a little bit more of a breeze. (*Beat*) Oh, and I could even hold the bottom of the steps for ya', if ya' like luv?

Carol stands there shaking her head.

CAROL: Brian Cooper, ya' ought to be ashamed of yerself. I mean, ya' must think that I fell off a flamin' Christmas tree, 'cos I can already feel ya' eyes burnin' a hole in mi knickers from here!

JACK: Hey, now come on Carol, ya' can't blame the lad for tryin', now can ya?

CAROL: No, I suppose not, but it's true what they say; the older they get, the worse they get.

BRIAN: I'll tell thee what, Carol. There might be snow on't roof, but there's a fire down below.

CAROL: Oh my God! Did ya' 'ave to go and put a thought like that in mi head, Brian.

Enter Kate, one of the other barmaids.

KATE: Er... What's up wi' you, Brian? Only don't tell mi that our Carol's still 'ankerin' after ya' body luv?

Carol laughs loudly.

CAROL: Aye, for medical research perhaps but for bugger all else.

KATE: Ay' up there, Jack. How's your Stella goin' on these days? It's just that I've not seen her around for a while?

JACK: Oh, she's alright. Apart from the fact that she's just about drivin' mi round the *bloody* bend at the moment.

KATE: Drivin' ya' round the bend? Why, now what's she bin gettin' up to?

JACK: Well, if ya' must know, she's always goin' about the house in her flamin' underwear and our Jenny's even worse. (*Beat*) And do ya' know somethin', it doesn't seem to bother 'em that there's men in't house.

CAROL: Er... Well, why don't ya' let poor old Brian come round and experience it then Jack? 'Cos ya' never know, it might just do the old lad a bit a good.

JACK: Aye and it might just give the poor old lad a flamin' heart attack as well.

KATE: (*Smiling*) Ah, but just look at him though, Jack, 'cos who would a thought that underneath that quiet, unassumin' exterior lurked a seethin' mass of hot and uncontrollable passion?

Brian quickly looks behind him to see if he can see who it is that they're talking about. He then turns back round.

BRIAN: (*Looking surprised.*) Who, me?

CAROL: (*Shaking her head*) Aye, him who says, who me! (*Beat*) It's just, I've been workin' here for nigh on five years now, and in all that time, I've never once known him ask for anythin' that wasn't either right up there on the very top shelf, or right down there at the very bottom. Honestly, it's just like havin' a pair of eyeballs sewn on to ya' bra-straps and the bottom of ya' knickers.

KATE: Ya' mean, unless he comes in wi' their Vera, and then he doesn't so much as even look at ya'. In fact, it's just as if ya' don't exist.

CAROL: Yeah, but do ya' know somethin' Katie? I think he's all talk and no action, don't you?

KATE: Aye, happen ya' right.

CAROL: 'Cos, I bet if I were to come over here, like *so* and then put mi arm around him, like *this*. And then put mi hand on his left leg and very slowly start to move it, *up* and *down* and *up* and...

Brian quickly jumps up off the barstool.

BRIAN: Hey, get off ya' daft beggar. Christ, is that the time Jack, only our Vera will be wonderin' where I've got to. Hey, it's lucky for you though, Carol, that I've got to shoot off early, or otherwise, who knows what might 'ave happened?

And picking up his pint, he swallows it all down in one go.

CAROL: I knew it; I flamin' well knew it! 'Cos he's all talk and no action!

BRIAN: Hey, take care of theesen Jack and I'll see thee on Wednesday night. Oh, and don't forget to remember mi to your Dot, will ya'?

JACK: No, don't worry, I won't. Now you take care of thee sen, lad, and don't do anythin' that I wouldn't do.

BRIAN: Well, that doesn't leave mi wi' much of a choice, now does it Jack? (*Beat*) Oh, and as for you, Carol, I'll deal wi' you later.

CAROL: Oh, promises, promises.

KATE: Hey, I'd hurry up and get off home if I were you, Brian, 'cos, I bet your Vera's waitin' for her Cocoa, luv.

BRIAN: Now look, take my advice, Kate, and don't try to be too clever, 'cos it doesn't suit ya', luv.

Brian leaves, as Kate sticks two fingers up at him, and Jack finishes his pint and puts it back down on the bar for a refill.

KATE: (*Gesturing to Jack*) So, what about this one, Carol? I mean, what do ya' think he'd do, if you were to do the same thing to him?

CAROL: Oh, I think that our Jack's a totally different kettle of fish, aren't ya' luv?

JACK: (*Laughs*) Er... I tell ya' what. Ya' could always come over here and find out!

Carol looks at him for a few seconds and then smiles.

CAROL: No, somehow I don't think so, 'cos I might just find mi self a little bit out of mi depth. (*Beat*) Er... What do you think, Kate?

KATE: Aye, I think ya' might be right at that Carol, 'cos ya' know what they say, don't ya'? 'Still waters run deep,' and in Jack's case, I think they're right!

END OF SCENE 6

SET CHANGE   (LIVING ROOM)

SCENE 7

'BACK AT HOME'

Ricky's mum is sitting watching the television with Jack when Ricky comes home from work. So, not wanting any fuss, Ricky goes straight up into his bedroom, but as soon as Dot hears him come in, she shouts upstairs to him.

DOT: Er... Is that you, Ricky? 'Cos, do ya' want mi to make ya' a drink and somethin' to eat luv?

RICKY: No, no thanks mam, I'm not really hungry at the moment.

DOT: Oh, alright luv, I'll make ya' somethin' later on then, shall I?

RICKY: Yeah, okay mam.

Dot goes back to watching the television.

JACK: Ya' spoil that lad, ya' know? (*Beat*) Only by the time you've finished wi' him, he'll be no *bloody* good to nobody. 'Cos ya' just a *bloody* fool, that's what you are. I mean, how many times 'ave I got to...

DOT: Oh, for *goodness sake*, Jack, why don't ya' just *shut up* and give ya' big fat arse a chance, 'cos ya' don't miss a flamin' trick do ya'? (*Beat*) No, it's any little opportunity to 'ave a go at anythin' or anybody, that's you.

JACK: *Oi!* One day missus, ya' goin' to go too far and then you'll get the biggest good hidin' you've ever had, if ya' ever talk to mi like that again. Do ya' hear?

DOT: Yes, and you do ya' miserable bugger, and it'll be the last thing that ya' ever do in this house, let mi tell ya'!

Enter Stella.

STELLA: Hey, what's goin' on? 'Cos, ya' can hear you two fallin' out halfway down the *bloody* street. So, what the *hell* are ya' fallin' out about this time? As if I didn't know!

Jack quickly stands up and slaps her really hard right across the face, sending her flying across the room, where she lands in a heap on the floor.

JACK: Don't you ever, ever, come in here shoutin' at mi like that again young lady, or you'll get some more of that. (*Beat*) Now go on; get out of mi *bloody* sight before I give ya' another one.

Stella immediately bursts into tears as she rushes out of the room and goes straight upstairs to her bedroom.

DOT: *My God!* Just who the *bloody hell* do ya' think ya' are? 'Cos I'll tell ya' this much, ya' not the man I married, that's for sure. And do ya' want to know somethin' else? I'm ashamed of ya', I really am. Call ya' self a man, ya' don't deserve to 'ave a lovely daughter like our Stella, ya' really don't.

On hearing all the commotion, Ricky comes rushing in to see what's happened.

RICKY: Er... What's up mam and why is our…?

Jack pushes past him on his way out of the room.

JACK: I'm goin' down the pub and when I get back you lot had better be on ya' best behaviour, or God help ya'; that's all I can say.

Jack goes out the front door, slamming it behind him, as Dot bursts into tears and Ricky goes over to try and comfort her.

RICKY: Hey, come on mam; don't go gettin' yersen all up set, 'cos he's not worth it.

DOT: Now look, Ricky, I don't want to hear ya' talkin' bad about yer dad like that, 'cos he's under a lot of pressure at the moment. What wi' him bein' out of work and wi' not enough money comin' in to pay the bills.

RICKY: Yeah, well I know all about that mam, 'cos I'm not stupid ya' know. But that still doesn't give him the right to go treatin' ya' the way he does. I mean, it's not your fault is it?

DOT: No, I know it in't, but like I said, ya' dad's not well and I know that ya' don't understand 'cos ya' too young, but one day ya' will.

Dot suddenly notices the envelope on top of the mantelpiece.

Oh, I nearly forgot luv. Somebody posted a letter through the door at dinner time and, I'm not sure, but I think it's for you, 'Lover Boy.'

Dot picks up the envelope and passes it to Ricky.

'the songwriter'

RICKY: Hey, wait a minute, 'ave ya' opened it mam?

DOT: Yes, of course I 'ave luv, 'cos I didn't know who it was for, now did I? After all, all it said on the envelope was, '*To Lover Boy*', so I thought it might 'ave bin for ya' dad.

RICKY: *(The audience can hear the contents of the letter, even though Ricky is reading it to himself)*

Hi there lover boy, I'm sorry but I couldn't talk to you earlier on today at work, because of Johnny. But if you still want to see me, then I'll be in the Four Seasons coffee bar, at 9 o'clock tonight.
Love Sheila xxx

DOT: So, who is it from? Anyone I know?

RICKY: Oh, it's just a friend from work, that's all.

DOT: *(Laughing)* Oh, I see, it's just a friend is it!

RICKY: Er... What's up wi' you?

Dot tries her best to stop laughing, but it isn't easy.

DOT: Oh, nothin', nothin' at all.

END OF SCENE 7

SET CHANGE   (COFFEE BAR)

SCENE 8

'DOWN AT THE COFFEE BAR'

Walking into the coffee bar, Ricky finds all his mates standing around the jukebox, taking the piss out of each other, while Barry, one of Ricky's other mates, who is a bit of a comedian, is standing with his arms wrapped around himself, as if he's kissing somebody. This is supposed to be a reference to Ricky and Sheila, which obviously makes everyone laugh; well all except Ricky that is. Now as soon as Ricky walks in, his sister,

Stella, grabs hold of the sleeve of his jacket and quickly pulls him over to one side.

STELLA: Hey, Ricky, come over here 'cos I want to 'ave a word wi' ya'.

RICKY: *Oh shit!* I'd forgotten that you worked here. (*Beat*) *Oi!* And that's mi new jacket when you've finished pullin' at it. Now let go of it, will ya'!

STELLA: Well, come over here then 'cos I can't talk to ya', if ya' keep pullin' away from mi all the time.

RICKY: *Yeh alright!* But watch what yer doin' to mi flamin' jacket, can't ya'. 'Cos look, ya' gettin' it all creased up.

STELLA: Watch what I'm doin'? Hey, that's a laugh, only it's what you're doin' that's worryin' mi, you *idiot!*

RICKY: Er... What are ya' goin' on about now?

Stella pulls him even closer to her.

STELLA: *Listen!* You're seein' Sheila Burton, aren't ya?

RICKY: So, what if I am? What's it got to do wi' you? 'Cos yer not mi bleedin' mother, are ya'?

STELLA: Er... I'll tell ya' what it's got to do wi' mi shall I? Only, if Johnny finds out that you're seein' Sheila behind his back, then I could quite easily be goin' to your funeral and I'm not jokin' either. So, just stop bein' such a *bloody* fool will ya' and leave well alone, before ya' go and get yer head bashed in!

RICKY: Hey, I can look after misen. I don't need you to tell mi what to do.

STELLA: Oh, well, if that's ya' attitude, go ahead and get yersen killed. But don't say that I didn't warn ya, that's all.

Stella goes back to serving her customers, and Ricky goes to join his mates, who are all standing around the jukebox.

'the songwriter'

PETE: Here he is, Britain's answer to Casanova.

RICKY: Ey up lads, has there bin any new records put on't jukebox lately?

MICKEY: Yeah, there's a new one by Stormy Tempest and one by that new group, 'Among the Missin'.

RICKY: Oh, well I'll put 'em on then, shall I?

We now see Stella taking three cups of coffee and three sugar doughnuts over to one of the tables that Mary and Janet from the factory and Mary's husband, Burt, are sitting at. Burt is reading the newspaper.

STELLA: Here wi are, three cups of coffee and three sugar doughnuts. (*Beat*) Now, can I get ya' anythin' else?

MARY: No, that's all thanks. (*Beat*) Er... But wait a minute, Stella. In't that your little brother, Ricky, standin' over there next to the jukebox?

STELLA: (*Sighing*) Yeah, it is. Why, now what's he bin up to? 'Cos I don't mind tellin' ya' that he's just about doin' mi flamin' head in at the moment.

MARY: Oh no, he's not bin doin' anythin' wrong as far as I know. In fact, he's quite a nice young lad, in't he Janet?

JANET: (*Sighs*) Yeah, he is and I tell ya' what, he can come and butter my toast anytime he likes.

MARY: *Janet!*

JANET: Oh, I'm sorry, 'cos I really don't know what comes over mi sometimes.

MARY: No, it's just that he's startin' to get in wi' a really bad crowd down at the factory and he's also gettin' mixed up wi' one of the young girls from out of the office, as well.

JANET: Hey, and she's a right little tart, let mi tell ya'. Ya' know the type I mean, after anythin' in trousers.

STELLA: Oh, ya' don't 'ave to tell mi 'cos I know all about it, but what can I do? It's just I've already had a word wi' him about it, but he won't take any notice of me.

JANET: Well look, would ya' like mi to put him across mi knee and smack his cute little round...

MARY: *Janet!*

Mary shakes her head and then gives Janet one of her long hard looks of disapproval.

JANET: *Hey!* Once they start thinkin' wi' their 'you know what', then there's just no stoppin' em. (*Beat*) In't that right Burt?

BURT: (*Sighs*) Yeah, its bin rainin' all day.

Burt carries on reading his newspaper.

MARY: *Burt!*

BURT: (*Looks at his watch*) Er... It's nearly 9 o'clock.

Mary shakes her head.

MARY: Aye, I know just what ya' mean, 'cos my Burt used to be like that when he were younger, didn't ya' Burt?

Stella and Janet both look at each other, but neither of them makes any comment.

BURT: Er... Not for me, thanks.

Janet gestures over towards Burt and shakes her head.

JANET: Oh, do ya' know somethin' Mary? I'm beginnin' to think that there might be life after death after all.

MARY: Aye, I think ya' might be right at that luv.

As she kicks Burt under the table, which makes him look up from his newspaper.

BURT: *Oi!* That hurt, only now what 'ave I done wrong?

MARY: Oh, nothin', nothin' at all. No, you just keep readin' the obituaries 'cos one day ya' might find yersen in 'em!

BURT: Ha ha, very funny, I don't think!

The door of the café suddenly opens and in walks Sheila with two of her mates. She smiles across at Ricky, as they make their way over towards the counter, where they buy some drinks, before sitting down at one of the small tables over by the window.

PETE: Hey, Ricky. Look at who's just walked in. 'Cos it's none other than Sheila *hot lips* Burton herself.

RICKY: (*Sighs*) Yeah, I know; I arranged to meet her here.

BARRY: Ya' did what? Well ya' must want ya' *bloody* head lookin' at.

Ricky's mates start to take the piss out of him, because of his involvement with Sheila. But Ricky just laughs it off as he leaves his mates and then goes over to join Sheila and her two mates, at their table over by the window.

RICKY: Hi, Sheila, do ya' want a fag?

SHEILA: Er... No thanks. Only I don't want to get cancer, even if you do. (*Beat*) Anyway, ya' can't smoke in here, 'cos it's against the law to smoke in a public place now!

Ricky lights up a fag anyway, as Sheila and both of her mates start waving their arms about because of all the smoke, which also starts to annoy some of the other customers as well.

RICKY: Hey, if I want to smoke, I'll smoke. I mean, who's goin' to stop mi? Not mi sister, that's for sure. So anyway, what made ya' change ya' mind about seein' mi, Sheila?

SHEILA: Listen, for your information, it happens to be a woman's prerogative to change her mind. And, if ya' must know, I wanted to go out wi' ya' but I knew that Johnny, or his dad, wouldn't be too far away, so that's why I daren't say anythin' to ya'.

RICKY: Johnny's dad? Well, who the *hell* is he when he's at home?

SHEILA: Oh, ya' not tellin' mi that ya' don't know who Johnny's dad is, are ya'? 'Cos he's your foreman, you idiot!

Ricky tries really hard not to look too surprised by the news that Norman (his foreman) just also happens to be Johnny's dad.

RICKY: Hey, I don't care who he is 'cos it doesn't bother me. Only I'm not scared of anybody.

Mandy, one of Sheila's mates, quickly butts in.

MANDY: (*Laughing*) Well, ya' will be if Johnny Watson ever gets hold of ya', and I'm not jokin' either.

Ricky takes hold of Sheila's hand.

RICKY: Hey, come on Sheila, let's go and sit over there in the corner.

So Sheila goes over to the far corner of the room with him, to where it's a little bit darker and also a bit more private. However, they have no sooner sat down, when Sheila decides that she wants to go and get another drink.

SHEILA: Oh, I won't be a minute. I'm just goin' to go and get another coke.

RICKY: Well I'll fetch ya' one, if ya' want one?

SHEILA: No, it's alright; I can get mi own, thanks.

As Sheila is waiting to be served, who should come walking in, but Johnny Watson and four of his workmates. At seeing Johnny, Stella very nearly drops someone's drinks, although, she's not as surprised as Johnny is at seeing Sheila, who is supposed to be staying in tonight to wash her hair.

JOHNNY: *Oi!* What are *you* doin' in here? 'Cos I thought ya' said that ya' were stayin' in tonight to wash ya' hair.

Sheila has to think quickly, as she looks over at her mates to try and get a bit of support. Except neither of them is stupid enough to go crossing Johnny Watson, so they just keep quiet and leave Sheila to have to talk her own way out of it.

SHEILA: Who, me? Oh, I got bored watchin' telly, so when these two asked mi to come out wi' them, (*she gestures over towards her mates*) I decided that I might as well get out of the house for half an hour. (*Beat*) Only it's not a crime, is it?

Then, instead of going to sit with Ricky, she goes and sits with her mates again, leaving Ricky sitting in the corner all on his own. So Johnny buys a coke and goes over to join Sheila and her mates, but then he suddenly notices Ricky and starts to put two and two together and makes five.

JOHNNY: Er... Wait a minute. What the *bloody hell* is that little toerag, Ricky Beaumont doin' in here Sheila?

JANET: (*Shouts*) She's up to no good, Johnny, I'll tell ya'.

MARY: Oh, for *Christ's sake*, Janet! Keep ya' big gob shut will ya', or you'll end up gettin' us all into trouble.

JANET: Well, why should I? 'Cos I'm only tellin' the truth!

SHEILA: Hey, Mary? Why don't ya' take Gonzo out for a walk, before I come over there and knock her teeth down her throat.

MARY: See, now look what you've done, 'cos I told ya' to keep quiet, didn't I?

JANET: Why ya' cheeky young Madam, I've got a good mind to come over there and box ya' ears for ya'.

SHEILA: *Alright*, come on then! Only I'd hurry up if I were you, 'cos then ya' might just 'ave enough time to get down to't Welfare and catch your Derek out wi' that blonde bit of fluff from out of accounts. (*Beat*) In't that right, Mary?

JANET: Er... What's she on about, Mary?

MARY: Oh, don't go takin' any notice of her 'cos she's just tryin' to wind ya' up, that's all.

JANET: Hey, now wait a minute. 'Cos is there somethin' that you're not tellin' mi Mary?

MARY: (*Shouts*) I'll say one thing for ya', Sheila Burton. You've certainly got a *bloody* big gob on ya'.

SHEILA: Yeah, well I suppose I take after mi mam for that. Anyway, why don't ya' tell Gonzo to mind her own business and stop pokin' her big nose into mine. Ya' stupid cow!

MARY: What did she just call me? (*Beat*) Why ya' little... *Oi!* Let go of mi, 'cos I'll knock her *bloody* head off when I get hold of her.

Mary attempts to go over and sort her out, but Janet and Burt quickly step in and pull her over towards the door, where they then leave the coffee bar and go outside into the street.

Stella is watching Johnny, who in turn is watching Ricky. So, sensing that her little brother might be in danger, she decides that now might be the right time to go and rescue him.

STELLA: Hey, thanks for comin' to walk mi home Ricky, but ya' can go now if ya' want to. It's just we're a bit short staffed at the moment, so I'm gonna' stay on for a little bit longer to help 'em out.

RICKY: Are ya' sure? It's just I don't like the idea of ya' walkin' home on ya' own.

PETE: Er... Look, don't worry about that Ricky, 'cos I can always walk her home when she's finished, if ya' like.

STELLA: Oh, thanks Pete. (*Beat*) See, so there's no need for ya' to wait for mi now, *is there?*

So, now realising that he is totally outnumbered by Johnny's mates, he decides to play along with his sister's rescue plan.

RICKY: *OK!* I'll tell mam that you're goin' to be late then.

Ricky stands up and begins to make his way over to the door, but as he walks past Sheila's table, Johnny reaches out and grabs hold of his arm.

JOHNNY: (*Laughing*) That's right; you run off home to ya' mummy, like a *good* little boy.

Ricky turns to face him, so Stella quickly jumps in-between them both, in an attempt to stop her little brother from getting a good hiding.

STELLA: *Hey!* You leave him alone, Johnny Watson, and go and pick on someone ya' own size, or ya' gonna' 'ave mi to deal with.

Stella quickly pushes Ricky out of the way.

JOHNNY: (*Smiles*) Oh, well that sounds good to me, Stella.

Johnny then puts his arm round her waist and pulls her over towards him, as Sheila quickly steps in and slaps him really hard across the back of his head.

Oi! What did ya' do that for?

SHEILA: What did I do that for? I just don't believe you, Johnny Watson, standin' there pawin' other women, right in front of me.

JOHNNY: Hey, ya' know me, I'm only havin' a bit of fun.

SHEILA: Oh yes, I know you, Mr Johnny *two face* Watson, 'cos ya' a *bloody* liar and I wouldn't trust ya' as far as I could *bloody well* throw ya.'

Ricky joins a couple of his mates over by the door.

MICKEY: *Bloody hell fire!* That was close Ricky, 'cos he nearly caught ya' that time, din't he?

RICKY: *Listen!* I keep tellin' ya' that I'd take him on any day of the week.

BARRY: Yeah, of course ya' would, but do us a favour will ya', and just let us know which hospital ya' want to be taken to before ya' do, alright?

RICKY: Ha, ha, very funny, I don't think!

END OF SCENE 8

SET CHANGE   (LIVING ROOM)

SCENE 9

'JACK'S LOST ALL HIS DOLE MONEY'

The next day back at home, Ricky hears a loud crash in the living room and his mum crying out in pain. So he rushes downstairs to investigate.

RICKY: Er... Are ya' alright mam?

Dot is kneeling down on the floor holding her face and Jack is standing over her with his fists tightly clenched.

JACK: What the *bloody hell* do you want? Go on, get out, and go and write some more of ya' stupid *bloody* songs, 'cos that's about all ya' *bloody well* fit for.

RICKY: Hey, come on mam, you just come and sit yersen down over here, while I take a look at that eye for ya'.

JACK: *Oi!* You leave her alone if ya' know what's good for ya', or I'll…

Ricky stands up to his dad.

RICKY: Or you'll what? Ya' pain in the arse. Only we're feelin' brave now, are wi? Now that we've been down the pub and had a skinfull. (*Beat*) And so, now it time to go home and knock *four bells a shit* out of the missis, is that it?

Jack is completely stunned by Ricky's reactions as he watches him go over to try and help his mam to get up off the floor.

Look, what is it mam, what's happened now?

DOT: It's him, he's bin down at the pub all day and now he's gone and lost all his dole money on the *flamin'* horses.

RICKY: (*Said to his dad*) Is that true, ya' daft bugger?

Jack now has a face like thunder.

JACK: Hey, I told ya' to get out, didn't I? Well, now I'm goin' to give *you* a *bloody* good hidin' as well.

RICKY: Oh, no ya' not, 'cos I've got an even better idea. Why don't *you* get out? Go on, get out and don't *bloody well* come back.

JACK: Why ya' little…

Jack makes a lunge at him but Ricky is too quick for him as he steps over to one side and lets his dad go flying over the back of one of the armchairs.

Aaah, mi leg, I think I've broken mi leg.

RICKY: *Good!* 'Cos it's a shame that ya' didn't break ya' *bloody* neck. (*Beat*) Only I'll tell ya' one thing, if ya' *ever* so much as lay a finger on mi mam again, I'll kill ya'!

Ricky helps his mam over to the kitchen.

Come on mam, let's go into the kitchen and put a cold flannel on that eye. 'Cos I don't want to worry ya' but it looks to me like ya' might end up havin' to go to the hospital wi' it.

DOT: Er... But what about ya' dad luv?

RICKY: Oh, I think we'll leave the daft bugger where he is for now and let him sleep it off until tomorrow, don't you?

Well they haven't been in the kitchen very long, before Stella suddenly comes waltzing in.

STELLA: Er... What the *bloody hell's* bin happened here? (*Beat*) Hey, 'ave you done that Ricky?

RICKY: No, of course I 'aven't, ya' silly sod. It's mi dad, he's drunk again as usual.

STELLA: But whatever made him want to go and do a daft thing like that for?

DOT: Oh, it's 'cos he's gone and lost all his flamin' dole money on the bleedin' horses again. (*Beat*) Well, that and the fact that he's had too much to drink as usual.

STELLA: So where is he now?

RICKY: Who, mi Dad? (*Beat*) Oh, he's sleepin' it off at the back of one of the armchairs in the livin' room.

So Stella goes into the living room to take a look for herself and, as she stands there shaking her head in disbelief, Jack rolls over and groans a couple of times.

END OF SCENE 9

SET CHANGE   (BENCH IN LOCAL PARK)

SCENE 10

'JACK LEAVES HOME'

Next morning, Jack has finally packed his bags and left home. We see him sitting on a park bench, but he hasn't been there very long before Ethel, (Dot's best friend), comes walking by as she takes her dog, Patch, out for a walk.

ETHEL: Ey up there Jack. What are you doin' out here at this time of the mornin', all on ya' lonesome?

JACK: Oh, hello there Ethel. I was just about to ask ya' the same question.

ETHEL: Ah well, I always like to take the dog for a walk at this time, 'cos there aren't so many people about and it gives mi a chance to think!

JACK: (*Looking about him*) So, where is he then?

ETHEL: Who, the dog? I don't know to be honest, only I let him off his lead as I came into the park and he shot off like a flamin' rocket.

JACK: Aye, he's probably gone chasin' after a little bitch somewhere. 'Cos ya' know what they're like?

ETHEL: Aye, I do.

JACK: Er... By the way, how *is* your Jeff?

ETHEL: Oh, he went fishin' at 4 o'clock this mornin', the soft beggar. (*Beat*) At least that's what he told me anyway.

JACK: (*Laughing*) Aye, he always did like a little nibble did your Jeff.

ETHEL: (*Sits down next to him*) Well, are ya' gonna' tell mi what's up, or am I goin' to 'ave to guess? (*Beat*) Hey, you've not left home, 'ave ya'?

JACK: Aye, as a matter of fact I 'ave, but it's a long story, Ethel, and I don't want to go boring you wi' it.

ETHEL: Oh ya' 'aven't, 'ave ya'? So, whatever made ya' want to go and do a daft thing like that for? (*Beat*) Er... Ya' 'aven't bin doin' somethin' that ya' shouldn't, 'ave ya'?

JACK: Well, like I said, it's a long story, but I dare say we'll manage to sort it all out eventually.

ETHEL: Hey, now look, why don't wi go back to my house, where I'll make us both a nice hot cup a tea and then ya' can tell mi all about it, luv?

JACK: Oh, our Dot would love that, mi tellin' everybody all her business. No, thanks all the same, Ethel, but I know what I've got to do. (*Beat*) Anyway, don't forget to give mi regards to your Jeff when ya' see him, will ya'?

ETHEL: What, and 'ave to get up at 4 o'clock in't mornin', not *bloody* likely! Ah well, I suppose I'd better be makin' a move. Now, I wonder where that flamin' dog's got to. (*Beat*) Right, well, I'll see ya' then, Jack, so you take care and I hope that ya' manage to sort everythin' out luv. I really do!

JACK: Aye, so do I luv, so do I. (*Beat*) Er... Now ya' won't forget will ya' Ethel, that *mum's the word!*

ETHEL: (*Sighs*) Aye alright, I'll do mi best. (*Ethel stands up and slowly starts to walk away, shouting her dog, Patch.*)

Here Patch! Come on, come to mummy then. *Here Patch!*

END OF SCENE 10

SET CHANGE   (LIVING ROOM)

SCENE 11

'BACK AT THE HOUSE'

Dot can't stop crying, no matter how hard she tries.

DOT: Ya' know, I just can't believe that ya' dad's left home, I really can't.

RICKY: Look, just stop it now will ya', mam. 'Cos if ya' want to know the truth, then I'm glad he's gone. I mean, lets face it; all he was ever good for was gettin' drunk, arguin', and gettin' on everybody's *bloody* nerves.

DOT: (*Sighing*) Oh, don't talk so daft Ricky, 'cos, for all his faults, he's still mi husband and I love him.

RICKY: Well, I can't see why. Only I don't know what ya' ever saw in him to be honest wi' ya'.

DOT: Now you listen to mi Ricky 'cos I know that ya' don't understand, but ya' see ya' dad's not well and he simply can't cope wi' bein' out a work. Well, that and the fact that he's not bringin' any money home. It's just the problem is, he doesn't feel as though he's the man of the house anymore.

RICKY: Yes, well I know all about that, but it still doesn't give him the right to keep hittin' you and our Stella, does it?

DOT: No, I know it doesn't, but, like I said, ya' dad's ill and he needs our help. So, go on luv, finish ya' breakfast and then go and get off to work like a good lad.

As Ricky's going out of the front door, Stella comes up to say something to him.

STELLA: Hey, Ricky. You be careful at work and watch ya' back luv, 'cos Johnny Watsons not stupid ya' know. Only he could see that there was *somethin'* goin' on between you and Sheila, when he saw ya' both in the coffee bar the other night.

RICKY: (*Sighs*) Yeah alright, I'll be careful. Thanks sis.

STELLA: Bye mum, see ya' later.

DOT: Yes okay, bye luv and take care.

END OF SCENE 11

SET CHANGE   (SHOP FLOOR IN FACTORY)

SCENE 12

'TROUBLE AT FACTORY'

Ricky clocks on and starts work. A couple of minutes later Sheila comes out of the office and walks by, smiling and winking at him. So all the lads point at him and pull their index fingers across their throats, as if to indicate that he could very easily get his throat cut, if Johnny Watson ever found out what was going on.

LIGHTS FADE OUT AND THEN SLOWLY COME BACK UP AGAIN TO SHOW A LAPSE IN TIME.

A buzzer goes off, it's lunchtime.

'the songwriter'

MICKEY: Hey, come on Ricky, I'll race ya' to the canteen. Last one there pays for us teas.

Sheila suddenly pops up again, and pulls Ricky away into a quiet corner of the factory, next to one of the outside doors.

SHEILA: Hey, and where do ya' think you're rushin' off to, *Lover boy?* (*Beat*) Come on leave him and come an 'ave a bit fun over here in't corner wi' me.

MICKEY: *Oi!* Are ya' comin' or not Ricky? 'Cos I'm not waitin' all day, ya' know.

RICKY: Er... No, sorry Mickey, I'll catch ya' later mate.

MICKEY: Yes well, you just be careful that you know who doesn't catch ya', that's all.

RICKY: Look, don't worry, I know what I'm doin'.

At that moment, Mary walks by on her way up to the canteen and spots them making out.

MARY: Hey, Ricky? don't forget to put ya' 'mack' on, will ya','cos ya' don't want to go and catch somethin', do ya'?

SHEILA: (*Laughing*) Aye, well, ya' know what they say, don't ya', Mary? 'No matter how young a prune may be, it's always full of wrinkles.'

MARY: Ah, ah, very funny. Ya' know ya' ought to be on't television Sheila, 'cos then at least I could switch ya' off!

Mary sticks two fingers up at Sheila and walks away. It's just right now, getting her dinner is more important.

SHEILA: Right then, *'Lover boy!'* I think it's about time ya' gave mi a kiss, don't you?

Ricky laughs as he pulls her closer to him.

RICKY: *A kiss!* Hey, I want a lot more than a kiss, ya' sexy thing. (*Beat*) Oh, and while we're at it, where the *hell* did ya'

39

get that miniskirt from. Only I've never seen one as short as that before. I mean, ya' can see all ya' flamin' knickers.

SHEILA: (*Laughing*) Yeah, but that's what ya' supposed to do, didn't ya' know?

Johnny Watson suddenly comes crashin' through the outside door, on his way up to the canteen.

JOHNNY: *Hey!* What the *bloody hell's* goin' on here? And just what do ya' think ya' doin' wi' my girl?

RICKY: *Your* girl? Er... I think you'll find that she's *my* girl now, *sonny!*

JOHNNY: (*Laughing*) Ya' what?

RICKY: (*Angrily*) You heard, now *push off* before I start to lose mi temper.

JOHNNY: (*Pointing his finger*) Hey! Yer a dead man my son, and I can tell ya' now, that you've got a *hell* of a lot to learn about women. (*Beat*) Now, come over here Sheila.

SHEILA: Oh, please don't hurt him, Johnny, 'cos he's only a kid.

JOHNNY: *Oi!* Shut it if ya' know what's good for ya', and I'll deal wi' you later.

Turning round to face Ricky, Johnny suddenly belts him right in the face. Then he quickly unleashes another two punches to the body, as Ricky goes down like a sack of potatoes, onto his knees. Then before Ricky has time to get up again, Johnny kicks him twice in the head. But then, to Johnny's surprise, and although Ricky is badly hurt, he still manages to get up off the floor.

Hey, now listen ya' stupid prat, stay down or you'll regret it. I mean it, I'm not jokin'!

RICKY: (*Smiles*) Well, we'll soon see about that, won't wi? So, why don't ya' try this one on for size.

Ricky lets fly with a left hook, but Johnny ducks just in time and catches Ricky with a right-hand uppercut, which sends him crashing back down onto the floor.

JANET: Hey, why don't ya' leave him alone, ya' big bully, and pick on someone ya' own size.

As Johnny turns to reply to her, Ricky quickly sees his chance and, getting to his feet, he flies at him, knocking him over into a pile of cardboard boxes, where, after a bit of a struggle, they both end up exchanging punches, as they roll about all over the factory floor. Well, by now, all the lads have come out of the canteen to watch the fight and to egg them on.

PETE: Go on; *sock it* to him Ricky! (*Beat*) That's it, now stick the boot in.

Well, to everyone's surprise, Ricky manages to give Johnny a bloody nose and then, to their amazement, he actually seems to be getting the upper hand and starts winning the fight. That is until Joey, one of Johnny's mates, decides to step in.

JOEY: Here, take that ya' little toerag!

Joey kicks Ricky really hard, right in the middle of his back, sending him crashing to the floor in a lot of pain. On seeing this, Johnny quickly jumps on Ricky and tries to finish him off. But just as Johnny is about to deliver the knock-out punch, Mr Dickens, (the manager), comes onto the factory floor with Ricky's foreman. (Johnny's dad)

MR DICKENS: *My God!* What the *bloody hell's* going on in here Norman? (*Beat*) Only in all my years as a manager, I have never seen anything like this before in my... I mean...

Norman just stands there looking stunned.

NORMAN: Er... You leave it to me, Mr Dickens, because I can assure you that I'll soon get to the bottom of it, you see if I don't.

MR DICKENS: Well you'd better because, if the boss sees this, then we'll all be in trouble. In fact, if I know Mr King, then there'll be absolute *hell* to pay, if he ever finds out!

Mr Dickens leaves, as Norman quickly starts wading into them all.

NORMAN: (*Angrily*) *Right!* Let's 'ave ya' all gettin' back to work. (*Beat*) That is, unless ya' want the sack!

They all quickly scatter in different directions.

MARY: Hey, Norman, it was your Johnny that started it, ya' know. Not Ricky.

NORMAN: Well, I think I'll be the best judge of that, don't you? (*Beat*) Oh, and as for you, Johnny, you'd better get out of here and keep ya' mouth shut, alright?

JOHNNY: Yeah, okay dad.

Exit Johnny

NORMAN: Right, Ricky Beaumont, you've been nothin' but *bloody* trouble ever since the first day that ya' got here, so go and get all ya' things together and get out of mi sight, 'cos, as of now, *ya' sacked!*

Barry tries to speak out in Ricky's defence.

BARRY: Oi, Norman! It wasn't all Ricky's fault ya' know 'cos your Johnny was just as much to blame.

NORMAN: Oh, so ya' won't mind comin' to tell the boss that then, will ya'? *No!* I didn't think ya' would, somehow!

So, not wanting to get the sack, Barry reluctantly turns away and begins to get on with his work, as Ricky gets his things together and then starts to leave the factory.

BARRY: Er… Are ya' gonna be alright Ricky? It's just ya' don't look too good to me mate.

RICKY: Yeah, I think so. Except for some reason, I keep on goin' dizzy all the time. (*Beat*) Oh no, here wi go again!

Ricky collapses on the floor, so Barry rushes over to try and help him.

BARRY: Oi, Norman, I think Ricky's passed out.

NORMAN: Oh, that's all I *bloody well* need. (*Beat*) Alright, you'd better keep an eye on him, while I go in the office and phone for an ambulance.

END OF SCENE 12

SET CHANGE   (HOSPITAL WARD)

SCENE 13

'IN THE HOSPITAL'

The next day, Ricky starts to come round in the hospital, to find that his mum and both of his sisters are all sitting at his bedside, looking extremely worried about him.

DOT: Oh, you had us ever so worried Ricky, ya' really did. (*Beat*) Only what did ya' want to go fightin' someone as big as Johnny Watson for anyway?

RICKY: Look, don't worry mam, 'cos it'll take a lot more than Johnny Watson to put my lights out.

JENNY: Hey, accordin' to some of the other lads, ya' were beatin' him at one stage. (*Beat*) Well, at least until one of his mates kicked ya' in the back that is.

DOT: That's right our Jenny, you go encouragin' him, why don't ya'! 'Cos that's all wi *bloody well* need.

Sheila suddenly comes into the ward, so his mum and his sisters get up to go outside, to give them a bit more privacy. Although this is not before Sheila, Stella and Jenny have had the chance to exchange a rather long session of dirty looks between themselves. Sheila then looks at Dot and somewhat nervously attempts to acknowledge her.

SHEILA: Er... Hello, Mrs Beaumont.

DOT: (*Ignores her*) Er... I think it might be best if wi waited outside, don't you Ricky? Well, at least until Sheila's gone anyway. (*Beat*) So, come on you two, let's go.

RICKY: Yeah, alright, thanks mam.

Exit Dot, Jenny and Stella.

Sheila sits down on the edge of the bed, so Ricky reaches out to take hold of her hand, but to his surprise, Sheila quickly moves her hand away.

SHEILA: Er... Listen, it's no good foolin' ourselves, Ricky 'cos ya' know as well as I do that Johnny will never let mi go and next time he might kill ya'.

RICKY: Now look, I've told ya' before, you let me worry about that, 'cos I'm...

SHEILA: No, I'm sorry Ricky but, whether ya' like it or not, I'm afraid that I'm goin' to 'ave to go back to Johnny, and that's final.

Sheila stands up and starts to leave.

RICKY: But, Sheila?

SHEILA: Hey, I'm sorry, Ricky, but I'm afraid it's the only way.

Exit Sheila. And as soon as Sheila has gone out of the door, Dot, Jenny and Stella come rushing back in to see what's happened and find that Ricky is now looking really upset.

JENNY: Er... Now what's happened Ricky?

RICKY: (*Sharply*) Oh, it's nothin' important! No, she's just gone back to Johnny, that's all, and now she says that she's not goin' to be able to see mi anymore.

STELLA: Yes well, I didn't want to be the one to 'ave to tell ya' this, Ricky, but it seems that ya' the only one who doesn't know that Sheila Burton is nothin' but a little tart.

And, I know that it must hurt to hear mi say this but the fact of the matter is she only went out wi' ya' in the first place to make Johnny jealous. And, it's not the first time she's done it either, and I know that for a fact!

RICKY: No, that's not true and the only reason ya' sayin' it is 'cos ya' don't like her.

DOT: Well, if ya' want my opinion, then I think that she's too old for ya' anyway!

RICKY: Oh, don't talk so *bloody* daft. I mean, what would you know about it anyway!

JENNY: Hey, don't you dare talk to mam like that, Ricky. Only who the *hell* do ya' think ya' are?

STELLA: Look, Ricky, Sheila's done it before and Johnny knows that she's doin' it, 'cos I can tell ya' now that even he in't that stupid.

RICKY: Oh, for *God's sake* why don't you all just go away and leave mi alone? In fact, don't even talk to mi anymore 'cos I don't want to listen to ya!

Ricky then quickly turns away and buries his face deep into his pillow.

JENNY: Yeah, the truth is ya' don't want to listen, 'cos ya' know that our Stella's right. Only Sheila Burton is just usin' ya' to make Johnny jealous, and the sad thing is ya' the only one that can't see it!

There's a long silence as Dot and Stella both turn to look at Jenny, in total disbelief at what she's just said to Ricky. Dot then sighs and starts to shake her head in dismay.

END OF SCENE 13

SET CHANGE   (LIVING ROOM)

SCENE 14

'BACK AT HOME'

A few days later, Ricky has been sent home from the hospital, where he is now resting quietly on the settee. That is until he hears Stella and his mum arguing about something in the kitchen. So he goes into the kitchen to find out what all the shouting's about.

RICKY: *Oi!* What the *hell* are ya' arguin' about now? It's just ya' makin' so much noise that I can't hear the flamin' television.

Stella immediately turns and looks away.

DOT: (*Sighs*) Well, if ya' must know, it's ya' sister, 'cos she's only gone and got herself pregnant, 'aven't ya', ya' silly gal?

Ricky is so stunned by what he's just heard that he just stands there with his mouth open.

RICKY: Ya' what?

DOT: Yes, that's right, that's what I said; ya' sister's gone and got herself pregnant!

RICKY: Oh, don't talk so *bloody* daft, mam! I mean, she's not even goin' out wi' anybody, are ya' Stel?

Stella doesn't reply, as Dot sighs heavily and then starts to shake her head.

DOT: It's that Johnny *bloody* Watson, that's who it is. Only so help me, I'll *bloody well* kill him if I ever get mi hands on him.

Ricky starts to laugh.

RICKY: *Who?* Johnny Watson? Don't talk so *bloody* stupid, 'cos our Stella wouldn't be seen dead wi' the likes of Johnny Watson. Would ya' Stel?

Stella bursts into tears.

DOT: *See!* What did I tell ya'? 'Cos you lot must think I'm bloody stupid or somethin'. But hey, I know what's goin' on around here and especially in mi own house let mi tell ya', 'cos people talk.

Ricky sits down next to his sister and puts his arm around her shoulders.

RICKY: Hey, come on sis, stop ya' cryin' and tell her that she's wrong.

Standing up, Stella goes over and leans up against the fridge.

DOT: But that's just it, she can't, can ya' luv? No, she can't 'cos she knows I'm right, aren't I?

STELLA: *Yes!* Alright, it's Johnny Watson's. Now, leave mi alone, can't ya? Just *piss off* and leave mi alone!

Ricky can't speak because he's still in a state of shock.

RICKY: Er... Now just hang on a minute, 'cos am I missin' somethin' here? (*Beat*) It's just, are ya' seriously tellin' mi, that you've bin seein' Johnny Watson behind Sheila's back?

Stella pauses for a second before she answers.

STELLA: Yes, but what ya' don't understand, Ricky, is that Johnny doesn't love Sheila any more; he loves me.

RICKY: Er... I'm sorry, but I don't believe I'm hearin' this. It's just if Johnny doesn't want Sheila any more, then why in *hell's name,* did he beat mi up the other day at work?

STELLA: It's called *pride* Ricky! Ya' see, he doesn't want everyone to think that you took his girlfriend off of him, now does he? Plus let's face it; ya' didn't really give him all that much choice, did ya'? Goin' at it right under his very nose, wi' his girl and right in front of all his workmates as well. I mean, you've just got no *bloody* sense whatsoever, 'ave ya'?

RICKY: (*Sighs*) Yes, but why Johnny flamin' Watson, of all people? I mean...

STELLA: *Why?* 'Cos I love him, that's why! Look, like I said, he knew that somethin' was goin' on between you and Sheila that night down at the café. In fact, he even tried to get mi to warn ya' off but ya' just wouldn't listen, would ya'?

DOT: Well, I've known about it for a long time, 'cos I've seen the way ya' look at him, when we're down at the social club at the weekends. Plus, my friend, Ethel, told mi months ago now that she'd seen ya' together in the park but, as usual, muggins here didn't believe her.

Ricky just stares at his sister in what can only be described as a state of total shock and disbelief.

RICKY: No, I'm sorry but I don't believe it. I mean you and Johnny Watson, of all people?

STELLA: Look, ya' don't understand Ricky!

RICKY: Yes ya' right, I don't understand and that's what he said before the fight.

STELLA: (*Looking puzzled*) Er… What do ya' mean, that's what he said before the fight? Come on, what did he say?

Ricky pauses for a second.

RICKY: (*Sighs*) Well if ya' must know, he said that I'd got a *hell* of a lot to learn about women.

It goes quiet for a second, but then, to Ricky's amazement, his mum suddenly starts to laugh.

Oi! What the *bloody hell* are ya' laughin' at now?

DOT: (*Laughing*) Oh, I was just thinkin', that he *beats* you up, Ricky, and then he goes and *knocks* you up. So, I was just wonderin' what he's goin' to do to me?

Dot goes over and gives Stella a cuddle.

Oh well, it's no use cryin' over spilt milk now is it? After all, what's done is done and so we'll just 'ave to make the best of

'the songwriter'

it, won't wi luv?

RICKY: So, what about Johnny? What does he 'ave to say about it then?

There is an extremely long pause, before Stella can even find the words needed to reply.

STELLA: Er… Well, the fact is I 'aven't told him about it yet, but I know he loves mi; I know he does.

There's a long pause, as Ricky and his mum both look at each other but neither of them makes any comment.

DOT: (*Sighing*) Right, I suppose that we'll just 'ave to look after it ourselves then, won't wi luv?

STELLA: Oh, thanks mam, 'cos I thought ya' were goin' to kick mi out and that I'd end up wi' nowhere to go.

DOT: *What? Me*, kick you out! Are ya' crazy? No, it's true I wish you'd waited until you'd got married, but that's my little grandchild in there and so I'm goin' to love it, no matter who its daddy is.

RICKY: Er… Look, I'm not bein' funny, Stella, but would ya' like mi to tell Johnny for ya'?

STELLA: *What?* Over my dead body! No, I don't and if ya' so much as even think about it, Ricky Beaumont, then it'll be over your dead body. (*Beat*) No, I want him to want mi 'cos he loves mi, and not just 'cos I'm goin' to 'ave his baby.

DOT: (*Sighs*) Yes, well she's right Ricky. So, ya' just keep it to yersen for now and let things take their course. *Alright?*

RICKY: Aye alright, but he'll 'ave to know sooner or later ya' know.

STELLA: Yeah, but not from you!

Dot starts to pick up some dirty pots from off the kitchen table and then goes over and puts them in the sink.

DOT: *Right!* I think that you'd better 'ave a walk down to the Jobcentre, Ricky and see if there's any jobs goin'. Only if ya' don't get another job soon, then I think I'll 'ave to go out to work.

There's a loud knock on the back door and who should come waltzing in but Brian, Jack's best mate.

Enter Brian

BRIAN: *Hello*, is there anybody in? (*Beat*) 'Cos it's alright, it's only me. Ay up there, Dot, how are ya' luv?

DOT: Oh, not so bad, Brian, not so bad luv. (*Beat*) Anyway, how are ya' mi old lad?

BRIAN: Well, I suppose I mustn't grumble really. I mean, I could do wi' a bit more money, I suppose, but then again, who couldn't?

DOT: Aye, I know just what ya' mean.

BRIAN: Anyway, where is the old lad then? 'Cos don't tell mi that he's still in bed on a day like this, surely?

Dot looking puzzled.

DOT: Who? Our Jack? (*Beat*) Well, I wouldn't know would I, 'cos 'aven't ya' heard? He walked out on mi about a week ago now and I've not heard from him since.

BRIAN: *Get away!* (*Beat*) Oh, I'm ever so sorry but I didn't know anythin' about it, Dot. Only that really is a turn up for the books, I must say. Although, ya' must admit that doesn't sound like your Jack, now does it?

DOT: (*Sighs*) No, I know it doesn't and that's what worries mi, Brian.

BRIAN: (*Sounding concerned*) Oh well, that's torn it, 'cos what am I goin' to do now Dot?

Dot looks even more puzzled.

DOT: Why, whatever's the matter wi' ya', Brian? It's just, ya' look as if you've got all the troubles of the world on ya' shoulders, mi old luv.

BRIAN: Yes, well I 'ave! 'Cos who am I goin' to go fishin' with, now that your Jack's not here.

Dot, who had been expecting the worst, now lets out a huge sigh of relief.

DOT: Oh, for *goodness sake*, Brian, is that all ya' can think about, 'cos I thought it were somethin' *really* serious, the way ya' were talkin'.

BRIAN: But, what could be more serious than that, Dot?

DOT: (*Smiling*) Aye, happen ya' right, lad. Only I suppose that that would be considered to be pretty serious, especially in the little world that you live in.

BRIAN: Aye ya' right, it is, 'cos who's goin' to help mi get the hooks out if your Jack's not there?

END OF SCENE 14

SET CHANGE   (BOTTOM OF STAIRS)

SCENE 15

'SHEILA GETS A LETTER FROM JOHNNY'

Sheila is sitting at the bottom of the stairs, reading a letter that she's just received from Johnny, when her mother comes to see what's up with her.

MRS BURTON: Hey, now what the *bloody hell's* a matter wi' ya', 'cos you've got a face like a slapped arse?

Sheila quickly stuffs the letter into her pocket, but it's too late, because her mum has already seen it.

SHEILA: Er… There's nothin' a matter wi' mi mam. I'm

just tired, that's all.

MRS BURTON: (*Said in a funny voice*) Oh, there's nothin' a matter wi' mi, mam! (*Beat*) So, who's that letter from then, that you've just stuffed into ya' pocket? Mr Johnny *bloody* Watson, I suppose?

SHEILA: (*Crying*) Yes, it is, if ya' must know and I don't know what to do wi' misen, mam, 'cos he's packed mi in and now he's goin' out wi' somebody else.

MRS BURTON: Oh, is that all? (*Beat*) Well, I wouldn't go worryin' too much about him if I were you, 'cos I can tell ya' now that there's plenty more fish in't sea.

SHEILA: Yes, but ya' don't understand mam. I don't want anyone else; I only want Johnny.

MRS BURTON: Well, I never liked him anyway, 'cos he was far too shifty for my likin'.

SHEILA: But I love him mam, I really love him and I just don't know what I'm goin' to do wi' out him.

MRS BURTON: Then ya' shouldn't 'ave been such a flirt, should ya'? Always foolin' about in front of him wi' all them other young lads, tryin' to make him jealous.

SHEILA: (*Angrily*) What? I never did anythin' of the kind, I was just…

MRS BURTON: Look, don't try and deny it, 'cos I've seen ya' wi' mi own eyes. Only, what about last week, when ya' were out chasin' after that Stella whatshername's younger brother, and he's about half your bleedin' age.

SHEILA: No he isn't, he's sixteen. Anyway, don't mention that Stella Beaumont to me, 'cos it's her that my Johnny's gone off with. *The ugly cow!*

MRS BURTON: *Sixteen*, is that all he is? Why ya' ought to be ashamed of ya' self, Sheila Burton, 'cos yer nothin' but a cradle snatcher, that's what you are.

SHEILA: Oh shurrup mam, just shurrup and mind ya' own *bloody* business, can't ya'?

MRS BURTON: *Oi!* Don't ya' go tellin' mi to shurrup, ya' cheeky little cow!

(*Enter Mr Burton from out of the next room*)

MR BURTON: Hey, keep the *bleedin'* noise down can't ya', 'cos I can't hear misen think in here?

MRS BURTON: *See!* Now look what you've done, you've gone and woken up Robert Redford and ya' know he needs to get his beauty sleep. (*Beat*) Don't ya', sweetheart?

MR BURTON: Er... *Freda?*

MRS BURTON: Yes, what is it now my angel?

MR BURTON: *Piss off!*

MRS BURTON: Oh charmin', I must say.

END OF SCENE 15

THE INTERVAL

ACT 2

SCENE 1   SET CHANGE   (LIVING ROOM)

'THE PROPOSAL'

Back at Ricky's house, there's a loud knock on the front door.

DOT: (*From the kitchen*) Answer the door, will ya', Ricky?

RICKY: (*In living* room) Oh, why is it always me that has to do it?

Ricky gets a shock when he opens the door, because it's none other than his old sparring partner, Johnny Watson.

And what the *bloody hell* do you want?

JOHNNY: Er... Is your Stella in?

RICKY: What if she is? What's it got to do wi' you?

JOHNNY: Look, I know that ya' don't like mi, Ricky, and I don't blame ya' but I've just got to see her. So...

Ricky goes over to the bottom of the stairs and shouts.

RICKY: *Stella!*

There's no reply

Stella!

STELLA: What?

RICKY: There's someone here to see ya'.

STELLA: Well who is it, only I'm busy?

RICKY: Oh, I think he said his name was *Johnny!*

Stella comes flying down the stairs like a rocket, very nearly knocking poor Ricky over in her haste to get to the front door.

STELLA: Oh, come in Johnny, it's alright. Come on, wi can go into the livin' room.

Dot comes out of the kitchen to see who it is and gets a bit of a shock when she sees that it's Johnny Watson.

Er... Mam; is it alright if Johnny and me go in the livin' room to 'ave a little talk?

DOT: (*Sighs*) Yes, I suppose so.

JOHNNY: (*Nervously*) Er... Hello Mrs Beaumont.

Dot looks at him but doesn't reply.

DOT: (*Sternly*) Hey Ricky, don't you go causin' any trouble. (*Beat*) Are ya' listenin'?

RICKY: Hey, I won't, as long as he doesn't.

DOT: Well, just to be on the safe side, I think you'd better come and talk to me in the kitchen. Then I'll at least know where ya' are and what ya' up to.

RICKY: (*Sighing heavily*) Aye, alright mam.

There is no need for a scene change because the kitchen and living room are both visible on stage at the same time, so one side can be lit, whilst the other side is in darkness.

In the living room area

STELLA: Er… Johnny, I've got somethin' to tell ya'.

JOHNNY: Yeah, but I've got somethin' to tell ya' first.

So Stella and Johnny both sit down on the settee facing each other.

JOHNNY: Er... Will ya' (*Beat*) Er... Will ya' marry mi?

STELLA: *Blimey!* Where did that come from?

JOHNNY: Er... I don't really know but, will ya'?

STELLA: (*Long pause*) Yeah, alright then, I will!

JOHNNY: *Ya' will?*

STELLA: Yeah, I just said I would, didn't I?

JOHNNY: What, ya' mean, ya' really will?

STELLA: Yeah, I really will!

JOHNNY: Ya' mean, ya' really, really, will?

STELLA: Yeah, I really, really, really, will!

JOHNNY: Oh but that's great, that's really great.

Stella comes rushing into the kitchen, pulling Johnny close behind her.

DOT: Well you weren't very long, only whatever's a matter? Is everythin' alright, luv?

STELLA: Oh mum, guess what? Johnny's just asked me to marry him.

On hearing this news, Ricky very nearly falls off his stool.

RICKY: (*Sarcastically*) Oh, is that all! *Blimey!* I thought you'd won the *bloody* lottery.

DOT: Now that'll do, Ricky and remember what I told ya'. (*Beat*) Oh, but that's wonderful news luv. It really is!

STELLA: Er... Ya' don't really mind, do ya', Ricky?

RICKY: (*Sighs*) No, not if that's what ya' really want.

STELLA: Oh it is, Ricky, it is.

RICKY: Well, congratulations then and I hope that you'll both be very happy. Although, you'd better look after her ya' know Johnny, or ya' gonna' 'ave mi to answer to.

JOHNNY: Don't worry, I will. (*Beat*) Although, let's face it, I could beat you wi' one hand tied behind mi back, any day of the week.

RICKY: (*Stands up*) Oh yeah, I'd like to see ya' try!

DOT: Hey, now listen you two, don't start all that up again, or I'll knock both ya' flamin' heads together.

RICKY: Er... There's one thing about it Johnny. Ya' won't be able to go puttin' it about like you've bin doin', will ya? Especially now that ya' goin' to be a dad, in't that right mam?

It suddenly goes so quiet that you could hear a pin drop.

JOHNNY: Er... I'm sorry but I don't understand. Only what are ya' goin' on about now Ricky?

STELLA: Oh, ya' stupid prat, Ricky, and that's even after I told ya' not to say anythin' as well.

RICKY: Hey, I'm sorry sis, but I thought he knew.

JOHNNY: *Knew!* Knew what?

Then the penny suddenly drops.

Er... Wait a minute, ya' don't mean...?

STELLA: Yes, Johnny, I'm pregnant.

Smiling very gingerly, Stella waits to see his reaction.

JOHNNY: So, I'm gonna...?

STELLA: Yes, well I'm sorry, Johnny, but I'm afraid that it looks like ya' gonna' to be a dad.

Johnny suddenly goes very quiet for a few seconds, as he tries to take it all in, but then, to everyone's relief, his face slowly starts to light up like a Christmas tree.

JOHNNY: I'm goin' to be a dad! *Me*, a dad! Oh, I can't believe it, only mi mam will be over the moon!

STELLA: Ya' mean, ya' don't mind?

JOHNNY: *Mind!* Of course I don't mind, but why on earth didn't ya' tell mi before?

STELLA: Er... Well the thing is, I didn't tell ya' before, 'cos I wanted to be sure that ya' wanted mi 'cos ya' loved mi and not just 'cos I was goin' to 'ave your baby.

RICKY: Hey, now hang on a minute, 'cos I've just realised somethin'!

Dot looks puzzled.

DOT: Er... What's that, luv?

RICKY: Well, I've just realised that this idiot, is goin' to be my *flamin'* brother-in-law.

Johnny starts to laugh.

JOHNNY: Yes that's right; you are, *Uncle Ricky!*

RICKY: *Uncle!*

Dot points at him and starts to laugh.

Oh, so ya' think it's funny, do ya' mam? Well, I don't know what you're laughin' at, *Grandma!*

DOT: *Grandma!* Oh dear, doesn't it make mi sound old? I mean, Grandma Beaumont?

Stella goes over and gives her a cuddle.

STELLA: Hey, you'll never be old to mi, mam.

DOT: Oh, I do wish ya' dad was here luv, I really do.

Dot is on the verge of bursting into tears, when the kitchen door suddenly opens and who should come waltzing in but her best friend Ethel.

ETHEL: Hello Dot, I thought I'd just pop in to see how ya' were and to find out if you'd heard anythin' from Jack yet?

DOT: Oh, hello Ethel. No, not a dickie bird but come on in and sit ya' sen down luv, while I put the kettle on. 'Cos this lot were just leavin', *weren't ya'?*

STELLA: Yes, alright mam but is it okay if Johnny and mi go back into the livin' room?

DOT: Yes of course it is luv. It's just that I want to 'ave five minutes alone wi' Ethel, that's all.

Ethel starts to feel a little bit uncomfortable.

'the songwriter'

ETHEL: Well, if ya' sure, it's just I don't want to go and put anybody out.

DOT: Look, don't talk so *bloody* daft, 'cos ya' know that ya' always welcome in this house. (*Beat*) Er... Why don't you go and make ya' self scarce as well Ricky. Well, unless ya' want to stay and make us all a nice cup a tea.

RICKY: Er... Bye mam.

Dot laughs, as she goes and puts the kettle on.

DOT: Yes, I thought that'd get rid of him.

ETHEL: Anyway, how are ya' then luv? Are ya' feelin' any better?

DOT: (*Sighs*) Aye, I'm not too bad I suppose, but I do miss him though, Ethel. (*Beat*) I miss him *so* much.

ETHEL: Well, I can't believe that your Jack would just pick up and leave like that and, without sayin' a word to anybody. I mean, it's just not like him, is it?

DOT: No, I know it in't and that's why I'm so worried about him, Ethel.

Dot starts to have a few tears, so Ethel goes over to try and comfort her.

ETHEL: Hey now look, you come and have a good cry if ya' want to. (*Beat*) That's it; you let it all come out and then you'll feel a lot better afterwards!

DOT: But what am I goin' to do Ethel?

ETHEL: Now look, stop worryin', 'cos if I know your Jack, then there'll be a good enough reason why he's not been in touch.

DOT: Oh, I hope ya' right luv, I really do. Ey up, kettle's boilin', so let's 'ave a nice cup a tea and a great big slice of chocolate cake and then I'll tell ya' mi good news, shall I?

ETHEL: *Good news?*

DOT: Yes well, don't go blabbin' it about all over the place, will ya'?

ETHEL: (*Sounding hurt*) Who, me? No, of course I won't!

Dot pauses for a second.

So, are ya' goin' to tell mi, or aren't ya'?

DOT: Er... Ya' not goin' to believe this, but I'm gonna be a Grandma.

ETHEL: You're jokin'. Well I never, hey that's smashin'! Oh, I'm so pleased for ya', Dot, I really am. (*Beat*) Er... But wait a minute; I've just remembered what it was that I came round to tell ya'.

DOT: Oh, it's nothin' bad I hope; 'cos I'm just enjoyin' this little bit of good news for a change. (*Beat*) Only what wi' one thing and another just lately!

ETHEL: No, no, it's good news. You see, I just popped in to tell ya' that there's a house just come empty up on Ladybrook Estate. Ya' know, just round the corner from me and, as far as I know, nobody else even knows about it yet.

Dot looks so confused by what Ethel has just told her, simply because she doesn't really know what to do about it.

DOT: Yes, but what can I do about it? It's just that ah' Jack normally deals wi' things like that.

ETHEL: Hey, I can tell ya' this much, it won't stay empty for long, Dot. In fact, the last one was only empty for about a couple of weeks.

DOT: Oh, I don't know what to do, I really don't. I mean, what would you do Ethel?

ETHEL: Well, I'd get misen down to the Council Offices first thing in't mornin' and apply for it, that's what I'd do!

DOT: Aye, ya' right, I will. In fact, I'll get our Stella to go wi' mi. Oh, thanks ever so much Ethel.

ETHEL: Hey, that's what friends are for luv.

END OF SCENE 1

SET CHANGE (OUTSIDE SHEILA'S HOUSE)

SCENE 2

'TRYING TO GET SHEILA BACK'

Standing outside Sheila's front door, Ricky takes a really deep breath before he rings the doorbell. There is a slight pause before Mrs Burton opens the front door and then just stands there, looking him up and down.

MRS BURTON: (*Sharply*) Well, what the *bloody hell* do you want, Ricky Beaumont?

RICKY: Er... Hello, Mrs Burton, I was just wonderin' if I could talk to your Sheila for a minute?

MR BURTON: (*Shouts from the other room*) Er... Who is it, Freda, and what do they want?

MRS BURTON: (*Shouts*) Its Ricky Beaumont and he wants to know if he can talk to our Sheila.

Mr Burton comes to the door and quickly pushes his way to the front.

MR BURTON: My God, you've got a *bloody* nerve comin' round here, after what that bitch of a sister of yours has just done to our Sheila.

RICKY: Er... I'm really sorry about that, Mr Burton, but that was nothin' to do wi' mi.

MRS BURTON: (*Smiling*) Oh, so ya' sorry, are ya'? Well, not half as sorry as ya' will be, if ya' come round here again botherin' our Sheila. (*Beat*) In't that right, Bill?

MR BURTON: Aye, it is! Now go on, bugger off before I stick mi boot up ya' arse, and don't come back here again if ya' know what's good for ya'.

And with that, he slammed the door in his face, with a really loud bang. So, not to be beaten, Ricky picks up a handful of small pebbles, which he then starts to throw up at Sheila's bedroom window. After a couple of direct hits, Sheila comes and opens the window.

SHEILA: (*Angrily*) Well, what the *bloody hell* do you want now?

RICKY: Er... I just wanted to see ya', that's all.

SHEILA: Oh, ya' did, did ya'. Well, I don't want to see you, *ever again*. Do I make mi self clear? 'Cos, did ya' honestly think that I would ever go out with someone whose slag of a sister went and stole mi boyfriend?

RICKY: Yeah but that wasn't my fault though was it Sheila. No, it was nothin' to do wi' mi. (*Beat*) Only ya' told mi that ya' loved mi, when wi were down at the coffee bar the other night, didn't ya'?

Sheila laughs loudly.

SHEILA: *Me?* Love you? Are ya' crazy? Look, I was just doin' that to make Johnny jealous. I mean, ya' didn't really think that I could *ever* 'ave any kind of feelin's for a kid like *you*, did ya?

RICKY: But I love ya' Sheila. I really love ya'.

SHEILA: Look, why don't ya' grow up, you idiot? Only ya' don't even 'ave a job and ya' spend all ya' spare time writin' down stupid bloody songs on little scraps of paper and empty fag packets.

There's a short pause, as Ricky tries his best to take in what Sheila has just said to him.

RICKY: (*Sighs*) So, ya' don't love mi at all then?

'the songwriter'

SHEILA: Oh, gimme a break, will ya', 'cos do ya' really want to do somethin' for mi, Ricky?

RICKY: Yeah, of course I do. Only I'd do anythin' for you, ya' know that.

SHEILA: *Right!* Well, do mi a favour and, *go and get lost*, and don't *ever* bother mi again. 'Cos lets face it, Ricky, ya' just a waste of space! (*Beat*) Now, *piss off* before I go and shout mi dad.

Sheila shuts the window with a loud bang. So Ricky slowly starts to walk away but then he suddenly stops.

RICKY: Yeah, she's right; I am a waste of space.

Taking all the scraps of paper and empty fag packets out of his pockets that he writes all his songs down on, he begins to rip them all up into tiny pieces and throw them up in the air, where they all land on the floor. He then starts kicking them about, until they're all eventually blown away by the wind.

No money, no job, and no girlfriend and nobody wants to buy any of mi songs either.

Taking a half bottle of vodka from out of his jacket pocket, he starts to drink it, as he slowly makes his way home. That is, until he meets up with one of Johnny Watsons mates, who just happens to be selling some grass.

TERRY: Oi, Ricky, want to buy some pot?

RICKY: (*Stops to think for a minute*) Yeah, why not, only what 'ave I got to lose now anyway!

TERRY: Well, how much do ya' want?

RICKY: Er... Gimme' a couple of quid's worth.

TERRY: (*Laughing*) A couple a quid's worth? Look, are ya' stupid, or what? Only ya' won't get any for a couple a quid. (*Beat*) Er... Hang on a minute, are ya' pissed? Ya' are, aren't ya'? Ya' as pissed as a newt.

RICKY: So, what if I am? 'Cos what's it got to do wi' you anyway?

TERRY: And ya' 'aven't smoked pot before, 'ave ya'?

RICKY: Yeah, of course I 'ave; I was just 'avin' a laugh, that's all. Now, stop pissin' mi about and gimme' twenty quid's worth.

TERRY: Oh, okay, keep ya' hair on!

Terry takes the money out of Ricky's hand and gives him the grass and a packet of roll up papers. So, as soon as Terry's gone, Ricky rolls himself a joint and starts smoking it. The only problem is, as Terry had already suspected, Ricky had never actually smoked cannabis before, so he is, to say the least, quite surprised at the outcome of it. It's just, for some unknown reason, he can't seem to stop grinning and he's now so light-headed that he feels as though he could simply fly away.

END OF SCENE 2

SET CHANGE   (LANDING/BATHROOM/KITCHEN)

SCENE 3

'BACK AT HOME THE NEXT MORNING'

Ricky is woken up by the sound of Stella, hammering on his bedroom door. The only problem is, after smoking too much cannabis, Ricky now feels like shit!

STELLA: *Ricky!* Mam says breakfast's ready and so if ya' don't come down now, then she's goin' to give it to the cat. (*Beat*) *Hey* and why is this *bloody* door locked?

RICKY: (*Holding his head*) Look, *sod off*, will ya'. 'Cos wi 'aven't got a bloody cat, so just *sod off* and leave mi alone, can't ya'?

Ricky puts his pillow over his head, so that he can't hear her anymore.

STELLA: Well wi can soon get one! (*Beat*) Er... Hang on a minute; ya' 'aven't got somebody in there wi' ya', 'ave ya'? Ya' dirty little devil.

RICKY: Oh, hark whose talkin', 'cos I'm not the one that's gone and got misen pregnant, *am I?*

STELLA: *Oi!* You'd better watch ya' mouth, 'cos ya' not too big to get a punch on the nose, ya' know. Now, come on, get up ya' lazy little sod.

RICKY: *Alright! Alight!* I'm comin'; now *piss off* and leave mi alone, will ya'?

STELLA: Well, don't be long that's all and stop swearin', 'cos it sounds *bloody* awful.

Stella goes back downstairs, so Ricky unlocks the door and makes his way over to the bathroom, where after locking the door behind him; he bends down and runs his head under the cold-water tap.

RICKY: Oh, that feels so good!

When Ricky's finished in the bathroom, he goes back into his bedroom and gets dressed. Then he makes his way downstairs to the kitchen to get his breakfast. He very slowly pushes open the kitchen door.

JENNY: My God, Ricky, ya' look awful. Only 'ave ya' been drinkin'? Ya' 'ave, 'aven't ya'? I mean, just look at him, he's practically fallin' over.

Jenny's voice sounds like a sledgehammer to Ricky.

RICKY: (*Sighs*) Oh, shurrup will ya' and stop shoutin', 'cos ya' givin' mi a bleedin' headache.

JENNY: Well just look at him mam 'cos I bet he's bin down 'The Swan' wi' that lot from the coffee bar, 'aven't ya'?

Ricky lets out a huge sigh, as he leans forwards and points his finger at Jenny.

RICKY: *Hey*, and what if I 'ave, there's nothin' wrong wi', 'The Swan', and what's it got to do wi' you anyway, only yer not mi bleedin' mother?

DOT: No, but *I am* ya' silly lad. (*Beat*) Only what did ya' want to go and get yersen like that for, at your age?

RICKY: Oh, for *God's sake*, just leave mi alone, can't ya'? 'cos you lot never shurrup do ya', no, not for one flamin' minute. It's just, nag, nag, nag, nag, nag, only no wonder mi *bloody* dad left home, the poor bugger.

So Dot puts his breakfast down on the table in front of him. There's fried egg, bacon, sausage, beans and two slices of fried bread. Ricky takes one look at it, then jumping up from the table; he puts both his hands over his mouth and rushes over to the kitchen sink and starts being sick.

STELLA: Well, that'll teach ya' to go out drinkin', won't it mam?

DOT: Hey, now stop it, Stella, 'cos all ya' doin' is makin' it worse.

STELLA: Oh, I'm sorry mam but it's just that it's so funny.

DOT: In that case, ya' won't mind cleanin' the *bloody* sink out when he's finished then, will ya'? And then we'll soon see how funny it is, won't wi?

Two weeks later and things are slowly getting worse, because Ricky isn't eating properly and he's constantly being sick. So, both his sisters and his mum are really starting to get worried about him.

END OF SCENE 3

SET CHANGE   (COFFEE BAR)

SCENE 4

'DOWN AT THE COFFEE BAR'

'the songwriter'

Stella's working down at the coffee bar, when some of Ricky's mates suddenly come waltzing in.

MICKEY: Er... We'll 'ave two espresso coffees, two cokes and a couple of cream doughnuts, please Stel.

STELLA: Ah! Just the man I wanted to see. So, come over here, Mickey Smith, 'cos I'd like a word wi' you.

Mickey starts to look about him.

MICKEY: Who, me? Why, what the *bloody hell* 'ave I done wrong now?

STELLA: Oi, Mickey, watch ya' language will ya' 'cos there are kids in here.

MICKEY: Er... Sorry, Stel, I didn't see 'um.

STELLA: (*Sighs*) Anyway, forget about that for now, 'cos I want to ask ya' about our Ricky.

MICKEY: Oh yeah, how is he?

STELLA: Oh yeah, very funny. I mean, how should he be, after you lot keep takin' him down 'The Swan' every night and gettin' him pissed?

MICKEY: *What!*

STELLA: You heard! So, stop tryin' to play the innocent wi' mi, Mickey, 'cos it won't wash.

PETE: Er... Now hang on a minute, Stella. Only wi ain't seen your Ricky for about three weeks now, 'ave wi lads?

MICKEY: No! Not since he split up wi' that cow, Sheila Burton from out of the office.

PETE: Yeah, in fact, wi were beginnin' to wonder where he was ourselves.

BARRY: Yeah, *and* he owes mi two quid.

'the songwriter'

MICKEY: Hey Barry, shurrup will ya', ya' stupid prat!

BARRY: Well he does, and I want it back.

PETE: Oi, Barry; *shut it will ya!*

Stella looks at them all and lets out a huge sigh. It's just that she's not sure whether to believe them or not.

STELLA: Well, I don't know then, 'cos he's comin' home pissed out of his head nearly every night, so I thought that he must 'ave bin goin' down 'The Swan' wi' you lot.

MICKEY: No, he's not bin goin' wi' us Stella. Hey, maybe he's bin goin' down 'The Red Lion' instead?

BARRY: Yeah, but what I want to know is, when is he goin' to gimme' mi two quid back?

TONY: (*Sighing*) Oh, for *Christ's sake*, Barry, shurrup about ya' flamin' two quid, can't ya'?

STELLA: Well, I'm sorry, but I must 'ave got it wrong then.

PETE: Hey, that's alright Stella. (*Beat*) Only, if wi can be of any help, then you've only got to ask ya' know.

STELLA: Thanks, Pete but, now I know that he's not goin' down 'The Swan', I think I'll be able to sort it out for mi self.

BARRY: Er... I know that you lot aren't interested but, what about the *two quid* that he owes mi? 'Cos it's bin...

All the lads grab hold of Barry and drag him out through the door of the coffee bar and into the street.

PETE: Look, I'm sorry about that but I think wi just need to take him outside for bit, so that wi can re-program him Stella.

STELLA: (*Laughing*) Yeah, I see what ya' mean Pete.

END OF SCENE 4

SET CHANGE (RICKY AND STELLA'S BEDROOM)

SCENE 5

'BACK HOME THAT NIGHT'

As soon as Stella gets home from work, she heads straight up to Ricky's bedroom, where she then tries to open the door.

STELLA: Ah good, it's not locked.

Inside, Stella finds that Ricky is completely dead to the world, so she takes the opportunity to smell his breath, but, for some reason, she can't smell any alcohol on it.

Well, that's funny, 'cos I can't smell any beer on him, or any other kind of alcohol for that matter!

But then she suddenly kicks something under the side of his bed, so, bending down to see what it is, she finds a small tin box, which she picks up and finds, to her horror, that it's what Ricky is using to keep his cannabis stash in.

Oh no, not drugs, Ricky. Ya' stupid little bugger! Only now what am I going to do wi' all this lot? (*Beat*) Oh, I know, I'll flush it down the loo!

So taking his stash into the bathroom, she quickly flushes it all down the loo.

Right, well that's the last time you'll need that little brother, 'cos I'll see to that!

Stella then goes into her own bedroom and hides the tin right at the back of one of her dressing table drawers and then she goes to bed.

The next day, when Ricky goes to get his stash, he obviously can't find it. So he goes absolutely crazy as he starts tipping the whole of his bedroom upside down, but he still can't find it anywhere. However, Ricky has made so much noise whilst he's been looking for it that Dot has had to come upstairs to see what all the commotion's about.

DOT: Oh, for *God's sake*, Ricky, what 'ave ya' bin doin' to this bedroom? 'Cos it looks like a *flamin'* bomb's hit it!

RICKY: Look, where is it, mam? *Come on,* what 'ave ya' done wi' it?

DOT: Done wi' it? Done wi' what? Only what are ya' goin' on about now, Ricky?

RICKY: Look, listen to mi ya' *stupid* woman. 'Cos what the *bloody hell* 'ave ya' done wi' it? *Come on* tell mi what you've done wi' it, 'cos I really need it.

DOT: Now you listen to me, Ricky Beaumont. And don't you *dare* talk to me like that, 'cos I won't stand for it, do you hear? I simply won't…

Ricky pushes past her as he shoots off down the stairs like a rocket.

RICKY: Oh, bogger off mam! Just bogger off will ya' and leave mi alone.

Dot sighs loudly, as she stands there looking up at the ceiling.

DOT: Oh, what am I goin' to do Jack? (*Beat*) Whatever am I goin' to do?

END OF SCENE 5

SET CHANGE ('PARADISE LOST') (RECEPTION)

SCENE 6

'JACK GETS LUCKY'

We now see Jack walking into the reception of a small factory which is called 'Paradise Lost'.

JACK: Er… Excuse me luv but the Jobcentre's just sent mi up here for an interview.

KAREN: (*The receptionist*) Er… Is it Mr Beaumont?

JACK: Aye, that's right luv.

KAREN: Right, well can I just start by welcoming you to 'Paradise Lost', Mr Beaumont, and so, if you would just like to take a seat over there in the interview room, then I'm sure that Mrs Peters, the firm's Personnel Manager, will be with you shortly. (*Beat*) It's just I'm terribly sorry, but she's just had to pop out for a few minutes, but I'm sure she won't be long.

JACK: Aye, alright luv.

KAREN: Er... Would you like a cup of coffee, or perhaps you'd prefer a cup of tea?

JACK: No, no thanks.

So, Jack goes over and sits down in the interview room and, a few seconds later, Mrs Peters comes walking into the room.

MRS PETERS: Ah, hello there. I'm sorry to have kept you waiting. Only you must be Mr Beaumont?

JACK: Aye, that's right, I am.

Mrs Peters shakes hands with Jack.

MRS PETERS: Right, Mr Beaumont, if you would just like to come and sit down over here, we'll make a start, shall we? (*Beat*) Now, I've been taking a closer look at your application form and, from what I can see, it looks to me like you've been out of work for quite some considerable time now. (*Beat*) So, tell me, Mr Beaumont, why is that?

JACK: Why is that! Ya' want to know *why is that!* Well, I'll *bloody well* tell ya' shall I?

MRS PETERS: Er... Excuse me, Mr Beaumont, but, if you are going to use that kind of language, then I'm afraid that I'm going to have no alternative, but to ask you to leave.

Jack quickly begins to calm down, because at the end of the day, he knows that he really needs this job.

JACK: Look young lady, whatever this job is that I've come for, I can do it. 'Cos, all I need is for somebody to give mi the chance to prove misen, that's all.

MRS PETERS: Yes well, I'm sorry but I'm afraid it doesn't work like that Mr Beaumont.

JACK: (*Sighs*) No, somehow, I didn't think it would.

MRS PETERS: Now, it says here that you used to work in the Mining Industry. Is that correct?

JACK: Aye, I worked down pit for nigh on twenty five year, man and boy.

MRS PETERS: So, what happened there then? Why did you leave?

JACK: Ah, well it was like this. 'Cos ya' see they were only payin' me £2,000 pound a week for a three day week. Plus six months' holiday a year and so I just thought that I could find somethin' better! (*Beat*) Only, are ya' for real, or what?

MRS PETERS: Now look, if you're just going to sit there and be sarcastic, Mr Beaumont, then I'll have no…

JACK: (*Explodes*) *Oh, for cryin' out loud woman,* don't ya' read the *bloody* newspapers or watch the flamin' television? 'Cos they've just about closed all the bloody pits down and put us all on the flamin' scrapheap!

Mrs Peters lets out a huge sigh, as she takes off her glasses, cleans them and then puts them back on again. Then, looking across at Jack, she sits up straight and starts all over again.

MRS PETERS: So, that must be when you went to work for the Mansfield Brewery. Is that correct?

JACK: Well ya' surely not goin' to ask mi why I left there, are ya'?

MRS PETERS: No, Mr Beaumont, I'm not, because I know that they closed down.

JACK: *Good!* Only it's comin' to somethin' when they start closing down all the breweries and half of the flamin' pubs as well!

MRS PETERS: Yes, well I have to say that I'm really sorry to have to do this to you, Mr Beaumont, but, after giving it a great deal of consideration, then I really do think that you're probably going to be just that little bit too old for us to be able to successfully retrain you.

JACK: (*Loudly*) *No!* Ya' not sorry at all; and shall I tell ya' somethin' else, *Mrs Peters*? I could 'ave saved ya' all this trouble, 'cos I knew that that was what ya' were goin' to say two seconds after I walked through that *bloody* door!

MRS PETERS: Now look here, Mr Beaumont, I…

JACK: No, you look! 'Cos all ya' doin' is goin' through the bloody motions, so as to justify ya' own flamin' job!

The boss of the factory comes walking into the office.

MR SOIZA: Er… Excuse me, but is everything alright in here, Mrs Peters? It's just, as I was coming down the corridor I thought that I could hear raised voices coming from out of this office.

MRS PETERS: Er... Yes, everything's fine, Mr Soiza. So, there's nothing for you to worry about, because I've got it all under control now, thank you.

MR SOIZA: Ah, well that's good.

Mr Soiza turns round to look at Jack.

Oh, hello there, are they looking after…? Er… Wait a minute! (*Beat*) Oh my God, is it Mr Beaumont? It is, isn't it?

JACK: (*Looks surprised*) Aye, that's right, it is but I'm sorry, I don't recognise you.

MR SOIZA: Well, I'm Roberto Soiza. Only surely you must remember me Mr Beaumont because we all used to live at the bottom of your street.

Jack pauses for a moment, while he looks at him a bit closer.

JACK: *Roberto Soiza?* (*Beat*) No, I'm... Oh, wait a minute, not William Soiza's lad, surely? Only the last time I saw you, ya' were about this high. (*Gestures height with hand*) But yes, I can see it is now. Well I never, only you've certainly grown since then, lad.

MR SOIZA: Yes I have, haven't I and that's all thanks to you, Mr Beaumont, because my dad always said that if it hadn't been for you getting him that job at the pit, then we might have all starved.

JACK: Oh, go on wi' ya', 'cos all I did was tell ya' dad that there was a job goin' in the office. It was him that applied for it and got it, it were nowt to do wi' mi.

MR SOIZA: Yes, well, I'm sorry, but I don't believe that for one minute, Mr Beaumont. (*Beat*) Only what about all those envelopes with little bits of money inside them, which were pushed through our letter box every week? And all that was before my dad even got that job at the pit and I'm pretty sure that that was you as well wasn't it?

JACK: Now look, don't talk so daft, 'cos I didn't even 'ave enough money to look after mi own family, wi' out givin' it away to you lot.

MR SOIZA: Yes, and that's just what my dad said; he said that he didn't think it was you because you were struggling just as much as we were. And so he thought that it must have been someone who had got a bit of money.

JACK: Well, there ya' are then!

MR SOIZA: Ah, but I saw you Mr Beaumont because, when you came to post one of the envelopes, I was down the cellar getting some coal in for my mum. And as I was looking out of that little air vent, you know the one under the front door step. I saw you because, although it was dark, the streetlights just caught the side of your face, so I'm almost certain that it was you. It was, wasn't it?

Jack goes very quiet for a few seconds.

JACK: Hey, listen! I don't know what all the fuss is about, anyway 'cos it was only a couple a quid, that's all.

MR SOIZA: Yes, well, I said it was you and that couple of quid, as you put it, added up to nearly three hundred and sixty seven pounds because my dad kept a record of every penny, so that he could one day repay it, if he ever found out who it was that was posting it. And it was you all the time! (*Beat*) Er… But wait a minute, Mr Beaumont; have you come for the machinist's job on the shop floor in section 3?

JACK: Yes I 'ave, why?

MR SOIZA: Well, I'm sorry, but you can't have it!

JACK: Oh, well that's good 'cos I didn't get it!

MR SOIZA: Right, Mrs Peters; I know that this is going to be short notice, but have you filled the vacancy for a foreman in section 1 yet?

MRS PETERS: No, I'm sorry, Mr Soiza but I haven't been able to get round to it yet. It's just, I was hoping to be able to start interviewing candidates for it sometime next week, but...

MR SOIZA: Well, you have now because I want you to give the position to Mr Beaumont. (*Beat*) Oh, and he's also going to need a secretary, a company car and an office. In fact, why don't you give him one of the offices up on the top floor, next to mine? (*Beat*) Er... Do you know, something Mr Beaumont, I can't wait to see my mum and dads faces, when I tell them that it was you who was posting all those envelopes through our letter box, because my mum always did have a soft spot for you you know. So, what more can I say, except, welcome to 'Paradise Lost', Mr Beaumont, because you deserve it, and so now it's going to be our turn to look after you, my friend.

JACK: Yes but look, I only did what I thought was right. I mean, what was I supposed to do, 'cos every time I saw ya', ya' were either runnin' about wi' no shoes on, or wi' ya' arse hangin' out ya' trousers. And all I wanted to do was to try and help ya' out a little bit, that's all.

MR SOIZA: And you did, Mr Beaumont, more than you'll ever know, let me tell you!

JACK: Anyway, how is ya' mum 'n' dad? Ya' see, I lost touch wi' 'em when they moved away.

MR SOIZA: Oh they're fine; except they've gone back to live in Spain now. In fact, they've just had a new villa built, just around the corner from me.

JACK: Have they really? Well, that sounds pretty good to me, Roberto. Only I bet that it's really nice out there, wi' all that sunshine, in't it?

MR SOIZA: (*Smiles*) Er... I tell you what, you'll be able to go and see for yourself, Mr Beaumont, because as soon as we can, we're going to get you and... Oh, I'm ever so sorry but I've forgotten what your wife's name was.

JACK: Dot. Her name's Dot.

MR SOIZA: That's right, I remember it now. (*Beat*) Right, well, as soon as we can get it all arranged, we'll have Dot and you on a plane, so that you can go and see where they live for yourselves. In fact, you could stay over there for a few weeks if you like. (*Beat*) Now, how does that sound?

JACK: Who me, up there in an aeroplane? I don't think so. No, I don't think so lad.

MRS PETERS: Oh, don't worry about that, Mr Beaumont, because you'll be alright, I can promise you that. After all, it's just like riding on a bus these days.

JACK: Aye well, if it's all the same to you lad, then that's just what I'll do, catch a flamin' bus?

MR SOIZA: (*Sighing*) You know you haven't changed very much at all, have you Mr Beaumont?

END OF SCENE 6

SET CHANGE   **(COFFEE BAR)**

SCENE 7

'A TRIP INTO TOWN TO BUY MORE POT'

Ricky goes into town to try to get some more pot from one of his mates down at the coffee bar.

RICKY: Hey, Tony! I don't suppose ya' could lend me a fix until tomorrow, could ya' mate?

TONY: No I'm sorry, Ricky. I'm all out at the moment, but I tell ya' what, why don't ya' try mi again on Friday, 'cos I might 'ave some by then.

RICKY: Well listen, I'll tell ya' what, lend mi thirty quid and I'll give ya' forty back on Thursday, when I get mi giro.

TONY: Thirty quid? I ain't got thirty quid. In fact, you'll be lucky if I can find thirty bloody pence on a Monday mate.

RICKY: (*Turns to Mickey*) What about you, Mickey, 'ave you got a fix, or thirty quid to lend mi for a couple a days? Only I promise I'll pay it ya' back, honest!

MICKEY: Er... Are ya' takin' the piss man, or what? 'Cos if I had thirty quid, do ya' think I'd be hangin' about round here all flamin' day, scroungin' fags off people?

Ricky doesn't know it yet, but Stella's already beaten him to it because she's been to see all his mates and told them not to give him any more drugs, or she'll report them to the police.

Ricky stops to think about it for a few seconds.

RICKY: *Stella!* Yes that's it; I'll go and ask our Stella, 'cos I know she'll help mi out.

Ricky quickly leaves his mates and goes over to where Stella is serving behind the counter in the coffee bar.

Hey Stella, I need to ask ya' somethin'.

STELLA: Er… Wait a minute Ricky, I'm just in the middle of servin' someone at the moment.

RICKY: Hey, Stella! I'm talkin' to ya'!

STELLA: Yes, I know you are but I'm servin' somebody, so you'll just 'ave to wait ya' turn.

RICKY: Look, for *Christ's sake*, Stella, this is important!

STELLA: Oh, for *goodness sake*, Ricky. What is it that's so important that it can't wait for just a few minutes?

RICKY: Er... Can ya' lend mi thirty quid?

STELLA: *No!* Now does that answer ya' question, or do I 'ave to spell it out for ya'? Now, go away and leave mi alone 'cos I've got work to do!

RICKY: Hey, come on Stel, I'll give it ya' back next week. Pleeease sis, only I really need it.

Stella stops what she is doing and just stands there looking at him.

STELLA: What! So that ya' can go out and buy some more drugs wi' it?

Ricky then has to stop and think about what she's said for a few seconds, but then the penny suddenly drops.

RICKY: Go and buy some more... (*Beat*) *Oh*, it was you that took mi stash, wasn't it? You *bitch*, you...

STELLA: Yes, I took it and I flushed it all down the loo and, I'll tell ya' somethin' else. If I find any more, then I'll do the same thing wi' that as well, ya' stupid prat! (*Beat*) I mean, I thought ya' had more sense than that, Ricky, I really did!

Ricky goes absolutely crazy, as he starts pacing up and down in front of the counter.

RICKY: You *bitch*, you *stupid bitch!* 'Cos I needed that, I *really* needed that.

STELLA: (*Smiling*) No, not any more ya' don't and if I see ya' wi' any, then I'll call the police. (*Beat*) Oh, and it's no use ya' goin' round all ya' mates either, 'cos I've already told 'em not to give ya' any.

RICKY: *What!* You'd report ya' own brother to the pigs? (*Beat*) Yeah, and I believe ya' would as well, wouldn't ya'? Ya' *stupid* bitch!

Ricky knocks some chairs over as he runs out of the coffee bar and quickly makes his way back home.

END OF SCENE 7

SET CHANGE   (LIVING ROOM)

SCENE 8

'BACK AT HOME'

When Ricky gets back home, he finds that his mum isn't in, but she's left a note, saying that she's just nipped out to the shops. Ricky picks up the note and then proceeds to read it out loud.

RICKY: Gone to the shops; won't be long. There's a trifle in the fridge but don't eat it all. Love mum x.

Ricky goes over to the kitchen draw and takes out a pair of scissors and a length of nylon rope from out of the cupboard, which his mum uses as a spare washing line. He then goes up the stairs to his bedroom, taking the scissors and the length of nylon rope with him.

Exit Ricky

THE LIGHTS FADE OUT AND THEN COME BACK UP AGAIN TO SHOW A LAPSE IN TIME.

Enter Dot

'the songwriter'

We then see Dot coming in through the front door carrying a small shopping bag. She then bends down to picks up a letter which is lying on the floor next to the front door. After putting the shopping bag down on the coffee table, she then sits down on the settee, opens the letter and begins to read the contents of the letter out load.

It reads:

Dear Ricky

Thank you for sending me a copy of the four songs that you have written. We have listened to them carefully and although we aren't too sure about the fourth one, we feel that the other three songs might be just what we have been looking for. So, subject to our legal department's full agreement, we've decided that we would like to offer you a recording contract.
We would therefore be grateful if you would contact this office as soon as possible, so that we can arrange for an interview with you.

Yours sincerely, W Anker

Dot smiles to herself, when all of a sudden she hears this loud crashing noise, which seemed to come from upstairs. So, she rushes over to the bottom of the stairs.

DOT: Er... Is that you, Ricky luv?

There's no reply.

It's just that you've got an important letter here, from one of those big Record Companies in London.

There is still no reply, so because it's such good news, Dot decides that she'll go up to his room and surprise him with the letter. Exit Dot, as she makes her way up the stairs.

END OF SCENE 8

SET CHANGE   (RICKY'S BEDROOM)

SCENE 9

'UP IN RICKY'S BEDROOM'

Dot pushes open Ricky's bedroom door.

DOT: Oh, Ricky, you'll never guess what you've... *Aaaagh!* No, no, for *God's sake*, noooo!

Dot screams because Ricky has hanged himself, by tying some of the nylon rope to the light fitting and then kicking the chair away that he was using to stand on. So Dot runs over to him and after putting both her arms around his hips, she tries with all her might to lift him up as high as she can, to hopefully be able to take some of the weight off the rope. Then, once again, she starts screaming and shouting at the top of her voice.

Help me! Pleeeease, for *God's sake*, somebody **help me!**

So Dot tries her best to keep shouting, whilst still keeping him lifted up at the same time. Well, Dot needed a miracle and that miracle came in the shape of Ricky's dad, who suddenly came rushing in through the bedroom door. Although, there was nothing that could have prepared him for what he was about to see.

DOT: Oh, quick Jack, do something! 'Cos I can't keep liftin' him up for much longer!

JACK: Aye, alright, don't panic!

So Jack quickly grabbed the chair from off the floor, and then standing on it, he lifted Ricky up with one hand, as he reached up and pulled the light fitting clean out of the ceiling. He then slowly lowered Ricky down onto the floor. Then after he'd got down and removed the rope from around his neck, he began to check to see if he could feel a pulse, but he couldn't find one, so he immediately started to try and give him mouth-to-mouth resuscitation.

DOT: Er... Are ya' sure that ya' know what ya' doin' Jack?

JACK: (*Sighs*) No, not really, 'cos if ya' want to know the truth, then I think he's a goner and that sadly, we're already too late.

DOT: Oh, pleeease God, not my little boy. Not my *Ricky!*

Jack then tries pumping his chest but, nothing happens. So he bursts into tears and sits down on the floor.

JACK: Look, it's no good, Dot, 'cos I'm afraid he's a goner and it's all my fault.

They both sit there looking at him, when to their amazement, Ricky suddenly starts coughing and moving his arms about.

DOT: Oh, *quick!* Do something, Jack!

JACK: Right, you'd better go and phone for an ambulance, while I check to make sure that 'is air ways clear. *Go on!*

Exit Dot, to go and phones for an ambulance.

Moments later, we hear the sound of the ambulances sirens.

END OF SCENE 9

SET CHANGE   (LIVING ROOM)

SCENE 10

'WAITING FOR NEWS'

Enter Dot and Jack, who have just returned from the hospital.

STELLA: Er... How is he, is he goin' to be alright?

JACK: Yeh, the hospital says that he's goin' to be fine, 'cos apparently, wi caught him just in time.

JENNY: Oh, thank God for that! (*Beat*) Hey and it's so good to 'ave ya' back home again dad, it really is. In't it, mam?

Dot suddenly bursts into tears, so Stella and Jenny both rush over to try and comfort her.

JENNY: Look, don't cry mam, 'cos I'm sure that he's goin' to be alright, now that he's in the hospital.

DOT: Oh, I do hope so luv. I do hope so!

THE LIGHTS FADE OUT AND THEN COME BACK UP AGAIN TO SHOW A LAPSE IN TIME.

A few days later, the phone starts ringing in the living room, so Dot stops what she's doing and comes rushing out of the kitchen to go and answer it.

DOT: *Hello!*

Pause

Oh, hello Ricky, how are ya' luv?

Pause

Yes, well I know that luv, 'cos Dr Ramjamful told us when wi' came to see ya' yesterday, that ya' could come home today.

Pause.

What's that! You want to know when wi' can come and pick you up! Oh well, I'm sorry but everybody's really busy at the moment. So, I tell ya' what, why don't ya' phone for a taxi?

Pause

Yes, I know that they're expensive, but look, I'll tell ya' what I'll do; if ya' get a taxi, then I'll give ya' the money back for it when ya' get here, okay? (*Beat*) Anyway, I'm gonna' 'ave to go 'cos I'm really busy at the moment, so bye and I'll see ya' later luv.

Ricky gets a taxi.

THE LIGHTS FADE OUT AND THEN COME BACK UP AGAIN TO SHOW A LAPSE IN TIME.

Enter Ricky as he arrives back home to find that there doesn't appear to be any sign of anyone there.

'the songwriter'

RICKY: *Hello!* I'm home.

But there's no reply.

Well, what a family! Only here's me, just got out of hospital and there isn't even anyone here to greet mi. (*Beat*) I mean, they couldn't even be bothered to come and pick mi up!

So, putting his bag down on the living room floor, he decides to go into the kitchen to get himself something to eat. However, when he opens the kitchen door, he finds that for some reason the kitchen is in total darkness, so he starts to fumble about for the light switch, when all of a sudden, it comes on all by itself.

EVERYBODY: *Surprise!*

Ricky very nearly has a heart attack because the whole of the kitchen is full of family and friends. Plus there's also a great big table full of, sandwiches, cakes, trifles and about twenty different bottles of, vodka, gin, whisky, rum and wine. Oh, and there's also a small barrel of beer as well.

RICKY: Oh, for *Christ's sake*, ya' nearly scared mi half to death! (*Beat*) Look, I'm shakin' like a leaf.

JACK: Hey, welcome home son.

Shouts his dad, as he goes over to Ricky and gives him a great big hug.

RICKY: Oh, it's so good to 'ave ya' back home again dad, 'cos I was really worried about ya', ya' know.

JACK: Aye, well, ya' can stop worrin' now, 'cos I won't be leavin' home again in a hurry, I can tell ya'!

DOT: *Oi!* Come over here Ricky and give ya' poor old mam a big kiss.

They all stand round hugging each other for a few seconds as Ricky looks at his mam 'n' dad and smiles.

RICKY: (*Sighs*) Hey, I do love ya' ya' know, but ya' know that don't ya'?

DOT: Yeah, of course wi do. But, what about this for some good news, Ricky, 'cos ya' dad's bin and got himsen a job, and he starts next week!

RICKY: Oh, that's brilliant news dad and I'm really pleased for ya'. I *really* am.

JENNY: *Oi! Ricky!* Look over here for a minute and, smile for the camera. (*Beat*) Oh come on, ya' can do better than that *can't ya'*! That's it, just *pretend* that ya' pleased to see us.

STELLA: Oh, by the way, Ricky, there's a young lady here called Ashley, who's just simply dyin' to meet ya'. Only ya' won't believe this but she's come all the way from her record company in London to do just that.

Ashley steps forward and holds out her hand for Ricky to shake. And so Ricky, who has now got the biggest grin right the way across his face, eagerly shakes hands with her.

ASHLEY: Er... I'm pleased to meet you, Ricky, at long last. You see, I've been asked by my record company to get you to sign these contracts. (*Beat*) Oh, and they'd also like me to wish you all the very best for the future, in your new singing and song writing career.

Now although Ashley sounds a little bit on the posh side, she also happens to be a little cracker.

RICKY: (*Smiling*) Well, it's very kind of you Ashley to 'ave come all that way just to bring mi these contracts to sign.

ASHLEY: Ah, well you see, I simply *had to come* and see who had written the songs for myself because, I thought that your songs were brilliant Ricky. (*Beat*) *Absolutely brilliant!*

MICKEY: Hey, nice one Ricky. I think ya' in there mate.

RICKY: Well, I'm sorry but I'm afraid there's just one small problem Ashley. You see, it's always been a family tradition, that before wi Beaumont's are ever allowed to sign anything important, wi always 'ave to kiss the person who has brought the documents to us to be signed.

ASHLEY: (*Smiling*) Ah, well in that case, we'd better not stand in the way of a family tradition, *had we?* Only, is this what you had in mind?

Ashley grabs hold of Ricky and kisses him, long and hard on the lips.

MICKY: *Woehayy!* (*Beat*) Well, you certainly didn't waste anytime, did ya' Ricky?

Dot starts to laugh.

DOT: No, he didn't did he, and that's 'cos he takes after his dad. (*Beat*) In't that right, Jack?

JACK: (*Laughing*) Oh, that's right; blame it on me!

BARRY: Er... Excuse mi for askin' Ricky, but what about the two quid that ya' owe mi? Only it's...

EVERYBODY: Hey, Barry. *SHUT UP!*

CURTAIN DOWN

THE END

IMPORTANT NOTICE

Would you please take the time to read D M Hopkins' comments on the next page, before attempting to embark on a production of 'the songwriter' as a stage play?

If you are considering making either a movie film, or a television play of 'the songwriter', then the following will not apply to you, simply because there is no live audience to have to consider. As after shooting all the scenes, you will simply be able to edit them all together in such a way that no-one will ever see any of the hard work that is involved, in all of the numerous sets and location changes that are obviously needed to make it into a successful film.

However to successfully perform 'the songwriter' as a stage play, you will need the use of a theatre, which is capable of being able to show all of the different rooms of the house, as being visible on stage, all at the same time. In that way, you will be able to cut down on the amount of set changes that are needed to successfully allow the play to flow smoothly and seamlessly through to its conclusion. Plus it will also mean that with the help of an experienced lighting technician, you will be able to simply light each individual room or set, as and when it is needed. I have been fortunate enough to see a full stage production of this play, which was produced in this same way at the fabulous 'Palace Theatre' in Mansfield and I have to say that it was absolutely fantastic to watch. Although I think that I should also say that as well as a strong cast, you will also be required to have an extremely experienced backstage crew, with lots of energy and enthusiasm for split-second timing and, above all, attention to detail. I only say this because this is, without doubt, an extremely demanding piece of modern theatre.

However if all this sounds so incredibly daunting, then don't worry because why don't you simply improvise and do it with just the actors and forget all about all the props and scene changes. I have also been to see a production of 'the songwriter' that was done in this way, and I have to tell you now that it in no way whatsoever loses any of it's magic! In fact, what I liked about it was, it also made the audience have to use their own imagination, which in my opinion, isn't such a bad thing anyway. So why don't you simply give it a try because you'll find that this play is so extremely rewarding to watch and to take part in, both as a member of the cast, or as a member of the crew.

scriptwriter/playwright D M HOPKINS

'the songwriter'

Director's Notes

'the songwriter'

Director's Notes

'the songwriter'

Director's Notes